REFERENCE

POLAND

Jay Heale

MARSHALL CAVENDISH
New York • London • Sydney

Reference edition published 1994 by
Marshall Cavendish Corporation
2415 Jerusalem Avenue
P.O. Box 587
North Bellmore
New York 11710

© Times Editions Pte Ltd 1994

Originated and designed by
Times Books International, an imprint of
Times Editions Pte Ltd

Printed in Singapore

Library of Congress Cataloging-in-Publication Data:
Heale, Jay.
    Poland / Jay Heale
        p. cm.—(Cultures Of The World)
        Includes bibliographical references and index.
        ISBN 1-85435-589-9 (vol.). — ISBN 1-85435-585-6 (set).
        1. Poland—Juvenile literature [1. Poland.]
I. Title. II. Series.
DK4147.H4 1994
943.8—dc20   93–45744
                        CIP
                        AC

Cultures of the World

Editorial Director	Shirley Hew
Managing Editor	Shova Loh
Editors	Tan Kok Eng
	Roseline Lum
	Michael Spilling
	Winnifred Wong
	Guek-Cheng Pang
	Sue Sismondo
Picture Editor	Mee-Yee Lee
Production	Edmund Lam
Design	Tuck Loong
	Ronn Yeo
	Felicia Wong
	Loo Chuan Ming
Illustrators	Eric Chew
	Lok Kerk Hwang
	William Sim
	Wong Nok Sze
MCC Editorial Director	Evelyn M. Fazio

INTRODUCTION

PERHAPS THE MOST REMARKABLE feature about Poland is that it is on the map of Europe at all. At least twice in its history, it has been erased and made part of other countries. Yet the Polish people remain. Today, Poles are busy shaking off the bitter memory of 40 years under Communist rule. Poland has emerged as a free country once again.

Rightly, it is a country proud of its past. In a way, it is one huge historical museum. You will find ancient forests and the remains of primitive people. You will see buildings, customs, and cultures that have clear links with Russia, Turkey, Italy, Germany, and France. You will meet a simple, proud, friendly people who enjoy life and wish to go on living. Poles are a resilient and cheerful group. "Two Poles, three opinions," says a local proverb! "Poland shall not perish as long as we live," says the Polish national anthem.

CONTENTS

Logger in traditional costume in the Tatras, a mountain range in southern Poland.

CONTENTS

In the spring, flowers like these wild daisies cover the mountains and meadows.

GEOGRAPHY

"THE MOUNTAINS, THE SEA, AND THE LAKES," say the Poles, to describe their country's attractions. These are the most dramatic features, although the heart of Poland lies in its spreading plains where the dominant colors are green and grey—green from the endless miles of small strip-field farming, woods, and parks; grey from the many apartment blocks, houses of unplastered concrete bricks, and industrial works.

THE SHAPE OF THE LAND

The country is roughly rectangular, stretching from the Baltic Sea in the north to the Carpathian mountains in the south. Its neighbors are Germany to the west, Russia to the north, the Czech and Slovak Republics to the south, and Ukraine, Belorussia, and Lithuania to the east. Poland is the ninth largest country in Europe—with an area of 120,728 square miles, it is slightly larger than either the United Kingdom or Italy.

Most of Poland is part of the northern European plain. More than 75% of the land

Opposite and above: **Tatra National Park and Polish farmlands. Green is one of the dominant colors of the countryside.**

is less than 650 feet above sea level. Poland's largest rivers, the Vistula and the Oder, rise in the Carpathians and wind north across the plains to the Baltic Sea. The central and northern areas are rather sandy and infertile. About 60% of the land is farmed, and over a quarter is covered by forests.

The capital is Warsaw, set slightly to the east of Poland's geographical center. To the north lies the Mazurian lakes and further northwest the Baltic coast. Southwest is the region called Silesia. To the south, bordering Czech and Slovak, are the Tatra and Sudeten mountain ranges.

SIX CLEAR SEASONS

Geography books describe Poland's climate as "temperate in the west, continental in the east." This is because far to the west lies the warmer sea air of the Atlantic, while to the east cold polar air blows in from Russia. Climatic conditions are important to Poland, as so much of the country depends on its agriculture.

Here, a blizzard blows, although in recent years Poland has had milder winters than usual.

There are six fairly clear seasons in Poland. Cold, snowy winter breaks into early spring, alternating bright and cold. Then comes spring itself, sunny and flower-filled. The short summers, with plenty of rain and sunshine, can be stifling hot in the big cities. Summer is followed by the golden, warm fall with rich colors everywhere, and then a foggy humid time heralding the approach of winter. The central plains are bleak and unappealing in winter, so people throng south to the ski slopes of the Tatra resorts.

Temperatures range from 76°F. or more in summer to 20°F. in the mountains in winter, although minus 29°F. was recorded in 1929. Summer can be very hot, with a record high of 100.4°F. The greatest amount of sunshine over the Baltic occurs in summer, and over the Carpathians in winter.

Rainfall averages 24 inches per year—from 31–47 inches in the mountains to 18 inches in the middle Polish lowlands.

A CARPET OF FIELDS

From the air, much of Poland looks like a carpet of narrow fields and meadows colored with the bright yellow of rape, the warm ocher of wheat and rye, and the fresh green of the potato plants—like a patchwork quilt made of thin parallel strips but without any dividing fences.

Before World War I, much of Poland's agricultural land was owned by rich landowners and worked on by their laborers. When the Communists took power, the government tried to enforce a policy of collective farms, but the Poles resisted bitterly the idea of joint ownership and sharing the proceeds. Only about one fifth of Polish farmland was collectivized. Young people worked in the towns, hoping to make money; old folk stayed on the farms. So, in the countryside, nothing much changed.

Today, freed of their Communist overlords, nearly three million farmers own 75% of the land. Their largest crop is rye—amounting to some 6.2 million tons, the largest rye crop in the world apart from what was the Soviet Union. Other crops are wheat, barley, oats, and sugar beet. Fruit, including blueberries, strawberries, and blackcurrants, is an important produce. Vegetables like potatoes, cabbages, onions, and beetroot are grown everywhere. There is grazing land and hay for winter fodder.

Most farmers keep at least one pig. Oak, pine, and birch trees line the country roads. The forested areas include larch and beech with spruce fir on the mountain slopes, although 79% is pine forest.

Vegetables are grown everywhere in Poland, and market stalls overflow with potatoes, cabbages, onions, beetroot, and other varieties of vegetables.

9

INDUSTRY

Poland possesses extensive mineral resources. Silesia in southwest Poland has one of the world's largest reserves of bituminous coal. There is sulfur near Tarnobrzeg, zinc and lead near Katowice and other substantial reserves of lignite (brown coal), rock salt, natural gas, and copper. Wieliczka, five miles southeast of Cracow, is the oldest salt mine in Europe and has been operating for over 700 years. So it is not surprising that the southwestern part of Poland is its most industrialized area.

The Upper Silesian-Moravian coal field is the second largest in Europe, exceeded only by the German Ruhr.

Residents of the town of Katowice live in close proximity to industrial buildings.

The old university town of Cracow, with the huge Nowa Huta iron and steel mill beside it, stands about 40 miles east of the main mining area. Wroclaw, another important industrial center, is on the Oder, about 90 miles to the northwest. Lodz is the center of Poland's textile industry: cottons, woolens, silks, and linens are all made there. Poland was, for some time, Europe's largest producer of flax and has a substantial linen industry.

NOWA HUTA From the walls of Cracow you can see a forest of smoking chimneys. This is Nowa Huta (meaning New Mill)—the Communist idea of "the workers' dream city." Slogans promised high wages, double food-

SULFUR IN THE AIR

West of Cracow is the old industrial center of Katowice, where coal, zinc, lead, and silver have been mined for hundreds of years. Today, large quantities of poor quality coal (brown coal or lignite) are burned to provide power for industry and heat for homes, and the air stinks of sulfur. The area is an ugly urban-industrial sprawl. Huge waste heaps and lakes of smelly water stand beside the mines and factories, while rows of grubby houses, schools, and shops fill the gaps between.

As a result, in Cracow the medieval buildings of sandstone and limestone are being eaten away by the polluted air. Sulfur levels are 250% above Polish safety limits and these are four times higher than those set by the United States. The Katowice region has the highest rate of stillborn children and birth defects in all Poland. A number of factories have been closed so as to curb the pollution.

In southwest Poland, among the forests near the border, stands the resort town of Jelenia Gora. This is one of the areas affected by acid rain, which officials say comes from across the border. The old forests were rich with spruce and pine. Now the trees are dying. Some blame fluorides washed out of the smoke; others say the soil itself has turned acid. Whatever the reason, the trees have fewer and fewer needles and eventually die. Where green forests once stood, grey dead trunks are all that are left.

rations, modern quarters, medical care … and "a dazzling unclouded future." The hopeful workers crowded in. They found themselves housed in huge, identical grey blocks, specially built with electric lights, kitchens and baths. As the steel works started, so did the pollution. Not a tree could be seen anywhere in this model city of socialism that was completed in 1954. Although it boasted 342 stores, 20 schools, and four hospitals, for its first five years there was no church.

The intention was political in building a huge steelworks so close to a city of historic importance. Cracow was a university town with very few wage earners. The state hoped to balance that situation by creating more jobs and thus increasing the number of workers.

According to socialist theories, workers should have the leading role in society. But Cracow wasn't a success. What happened instead was that the intellectuals of Cracow focused attention on the appalling pollution from Nowa Huta. If the wind blows toward the city, the stench of another failed Communist experiment is clear to every visitor. The people who live there know it all too well.

WARSAW

The greatest river in Poland, so they say, once sheltered a mermaid. Half woman, half fish, she can still be seen on the coat of arms of Warsaw.

This sadly historic city is surrounded by seemingly endless grey housing estates. Fortunately, the busy roads lead straight to the more attractive modern city center, around the landmark of the Palace of Culture and Science. The more historic parts as well as the newer residential areas are on the west bank of the broad Vistula River. The eastern bank is called the Praga: it escaped war damage because the Red Army occupied it before the Nazis could blow it up.

In Castle Square, the way into the Old Town, stands a slender column with the statue of Zygmund III Wasa, the king who made Warsaw his capital in 1586. This is Warsaw's oldest monument and was the first to be rebuilt after World War II. Horse-drawn carts clatter across the cobblestones, past the open-air cafés, souvenir sellers, artists, flower stalls, and camera-happy tourists.

Tourists visit the Royal Castle with its beautifully restored interior, the Historical Museum, and the Cathedral of St. John— the scene of some of the most bitter fighting in the Warsaw Uprising, when

The horse-drawn cart is a favorite with tourists.

12

A CITY REBUILT

At the end of World War II, Warsaw lay in ruins, a victim of systematic Nazi destruction. In a strangely uncharacteristic mood, the new Communist rulers chose to rebuild old Warsaw rather than build thousands of houses for the people. So, working from old prints and paintings, this historic city was painstakingly reconstructed. Paintings of 18th century Warsaw, saved from the burning ruins of the former Royal Castle, served as architectural models. Twenty million tons of rubble were removed and turned into building material. One hundred car-loads of rubble were removed every day. Women and high school youths helped in the rebuilding.

Today, the warm pastel colors of Warsaw's Old Town (above) exist once more, although the past has not been forgotten. There are memorial plaques everywhere describing mass executions of civilians, and bullet holes can still be seen on the few original sections of the rebuilt houses.

250,000 Poles were killed during two months of street fighting against their Nazi conquerors.

South of the city is the Wilanow Palace, once the summer residence of Jan III Sobieski, a 17th century king of Poland. Visitors to the palace wear felt slippers, obligatory in all Polish museums, as they view superbly painted walls and ceilings, and admire the formal gardens.

"This city will not rise again."

—German Commander von dem Bach

A network of hiking trails links the Tatra villages, waterfalls, and lakes. Climbing guides and a mountain rescue service are provided by the local highlanders, the Gorale.

MOUNTAIN RANGES

Poland's southern boundary is formed of mountains. Snow-capped for much of the year, the Tatra mountains are the best known and most popular. For hikers and climbers in summer and skiers in winter, these alpine-style heights offer year-round outdoor adventure. Rising to over 8,100 feet, the High Tatras are only one part of the Carpathian range that belongs jointly to Poland and the Czech and Slovak Republics.

Farther east, the Pieniny mountains are cut by the Dunajec river, and to the far southeast stands the Beskidy range, picturesque with spruce and beech forests, the source of the Vistula River, which flows across the Polish plain.

The mountains are not only there for enjoyment. Forestry is an important industry.

The foothills of the Tatras are called Podhale—a sparsely-populated region of lush meadows where the main town is Nowy Targ, known for its once-a-week market which starts at 3 a.m. each Thursday.

Deeper into the Tatras, past steep-sided valleys and quaint villages carved lovingly from the local timber, stands Zakopane, a little mountain town that attracts visitors from all over Poland and is a gathering place for artists.

CRACOW

Where the Tatra mountains join the plain stands Cracow, once the capital of Poland and the seat of Poland's oldest university, the Jagiellonian University founded in 1364. It is a completely preserved medieval city, the only Polish city to escape devastation in World War II. It is listed by Unesco as one of the world's twelve most significant historic sites.

The Rynek Glowny is the market square—once the largest square in Europe. Tourists sit at the sidewalk cafés drinking cups of strong Polish coffee. The local people stand and watch displays of traditional dancing or local music groups. Flower sellers surround the long medieval Cloth Hall, now a covered market full of booths selling folk art souvenirs. In the corner of the square stands the imposingly towered Church of Our Lady Mary.

Wawel Hill on a bend of the Vistula River is one of the historical gems of Poland. Here the Royal Castle of Wawel sits high on a hill above the Vistula. Rebuilt at the end of the 16th century, it boasts a great courtyard and a crypt where Polish kings lie entombed in massive marble. In the Wawel Royal Cathedral are buried all but four of Poland's 45 monarchs. Long lines of school children walk through rooms decorated in colored marble and hung with priceless Flemish tapestries, viewing such treasures as a jewel-studded shield captured from the Turks at the battle of Vienna in 1683, a velvet hat with a dove embroidered in pearls that was given to Jan Sobieski, a 17th century Polish king, by the pope after Vienna was saved, and a dazzling robe embroidered with heraldic suns similarly given to Sobieski by French King Louis XIV.

Legend has it that a dragon (depicted in the sculpture in the picture to the right) lived in a cave beneath Wawel Hill. Krak, the mythical founder of Cracow, killed the beast by feeding it animal skins stuffed with tar and sulfur. The dragon gobbled them up, was driven into a frenzy of thirst, rushed into the Vistula and drank until it exploded.

BALTIC COAST

Poland has a coastline 430 miles long, from which fishermen add 200,000 tons of fish each year to the Polish diet. There are good fishing grounds in the Baltic for cod and herring. But the water is not as clean as it used to be, and pollution has already killed off some species of fish, including the sturgeon.

Gdansk was once the greatest Polish city—in the 17th century its population of 70,000 was more than double that of Warsaw. But it has suffered more than any other city of modern Poland. The Russians destroyed 90% of it when they "liberated" the town after the German occupation. Gdansk was the birthplace of the free trade union, Solidarity.

Gdansk is linked by urban development to its neighbors Sopot and Gdynia, forming what is known as the Tri-City. The polluted waters of the Vistula enter the sea here, affecting the whole Gdansk bay.

To the east lies the Mazurian lake system, good for sailing and swimming, and highly popular in summer. The main launching point for canoeists and forest hikers is Olsztyn.

Go to Hel! Why not? The Hel Peninsula is a long thin strip of land jutting out into the Baltic. On one side are safe sandy beaches and 10 minutes' walk brings you to the waters of the Vistula estuary. In 1919, the fishermen of Hel, who considered themselves "true Slavs," voted to become part of Poland.

POLISH WILDLIFE

A land so full of ancient forests, tangled lakes, and high mountains has its fair share of exciting wildlife as well. Large mammals include wild boar, elk, occasional brown bear, and a few herds of the woodland-dwelling European bison. In the High Tatras, there are chamois and marmot.

On Poland's farthest eastern border, Bialowieza Forest is a national park of over 300,000 acres that once had one of the world's remaining herds of wild bison. During World War I, all the bison were killed by hungry soldiers. In 1929, three pairs of bison were returned to the forest from foreign zoos. There are now about 300 roaming there freely, along with deer, wildcats, lynxes, wolves, and beavers. They live in one of the last fragments of untouched forest in Europe. Their home among huge spruce trees that reach to 150 feet has been likened to a great green cathedral. Numerous national parks and conservation areas, with sightseeing spots, are protected and managed by the state.

The Tatra mountains have been a national park since 1954. Brown bears still live there, but not many.

According to the Committee for the Protection of Eagles in Poland, there are around 350 pairs of eagles, carefully watched to ensure that they have absolute quiet when they hatch eggs and look after their fledglings. The eagle is the national emblem of Poland.

Flowers—white daisies, scarlet poppies, and blue cornflowers—grow in the hedges and field corners where ploughs cannot reach. In spring, the mountains sparkle with alpine flowers. But perhaps the greatest natural beauty of Poland lies in the deep forests, especially in the fall when the low sun slants through yellow birch leaves and golden beech.

Opposite: Fishing boats at Sopot. There are good fishing grounds in the Baltic, but fishermen have a hard life.

This herd of bison lives in the Bialowieza National Park, part of the largest forest area of the Central European plain.

HISTORY

THE YEAR A.D. 966 is considered the founding of Poland, for that was when its Piast ruler Mieszko I adopted Christianity. During his rule, tribes speaking the same language became united. There had been Slavonic tribes living in the Vistula River basin since about 2 million B.C. but they migrated in many directions. It wasn't until the ninth century A.D. that several West Slavic tribes united to form small states. One became known as the Piast dynasty, which united the region round modern Poznan.

Those were the days when each local nobleman kept his own private army. With the countryside divided into dukedoms and principalities, the young Poland had its share of internal conflicts. But by 1109 it was strong enough to beat off a German invasion. A network of castles was built to defend the borders. Poland grew into a mighty kingdom, stretching from the Baltic to the Black Sea. When it united with Lithuania in the 15th century, Poland was the largest country in Europe.

INVASIONS

The geographical position of Poland, spread across the northern plains between Europe and Asia, made it the obvious route for invaders. In 1241, the Mongol hordes of Genghis Khan left trails of destruction behind them. The European knights were no match for them. Happily for Christendom, the Mongols did not try to conquer Europe. But they returned twice more that century, leaving most Polish cities burned behind them.

The Teutonic Knights were one of the three great military and religious orders that sprang from the Crusades, the holy wars between Christians and Moslems. Their initial purpose had been charity and care of the sick, but as their power increased, they became more cruel. In 1308, they snatched the lands of Pomerania, cutting Poland off from the Baltic and beginning 150 years of warfare with Poland.

Opposite: **Wawel Castle in Cracow, one of the many castles that were built when Poland was a mighty kingdom. Polish kings lie entombed in marble in the crypt of the cathedral there.**

HEYNAL TRUMPET CALL

In the center of Cracow rise the two Gothic towers of the Church of Our Lady Mary (left). The towers are uneven. Legend insists that the builder of the shorter one fell off and died, so in respect the tower was left at that height. The higher of the two towers is known as the Tower of the Cracow Trumpeter. The story is told of how a young trumpeter in 1241 sounded the alarm when Tartars began burning the city. An arrow pierced his throat—that is why, when the trumpet sounds today, the last note begins strongly, trembles and then ceases. Even during the German occupation, the trumpet sounded "every hour of the day and night." Men from the Polish fire brigade now have the privilege of sounding the trumpet. They still swear the ancient oath to "sound the Heynal each hour in honor of Our Lady in the tower of the church which bears Her Name."

In 1500, the Kingdom of Poland (then combined with Lithuania, Hungary, and Bohemia) was the largest state in Europe. Russian armies invaded, led by Tsar Ivan IV, "Ivan the Terrible," who was defeated by the Polish king Stefan Batory in 1581. Later, a cruel Swedish occupation of Poland (1655–60) decreased the population by a third. Such invasions continued when Russia, Prussia, and Austria took their share.

TO THE RESCUE

Jan Sobieski has the title "savior of the country." After winning two battles against invading Turks, he was elected king of Poland in 1674. He made a pact with Leopold I of Austria who, in 1683, called on Sobieski to save Vienna. Combining forces with Charles of Lorraine, Sobieski drove back the besieging Turks. Polish greatness declined after his death in 1696, and private armies ruled the land. The invasions of Tartars and Swedes had left huge areas unpopulated. Weakened by wars with the Ottoman Empire, disagreements among the nobles, and quarrels at the election of every king, Poland lay prey to the now greater powers of Europe.

POLAND VANISHES

In 1772 came the first of three partitions of the republic. Russia, Austria, and Prussia seized 81,000 square miles of Polish territory. Jolted into action, Polish society initiated a better education system, and encouraged by a wave of fresh political thinking, the people cried out for reforms. In 1791 Poland's Sejm (SAYm) or parliament adopted a new constitution—the second country in the world after the United States to do so.

But the envisaged consolidation of royal power and political reorganization brought fierce opposition from Russia, whose troops entered Poland. In 1793, the Constitution was abolished and a second partition was made between Russia and Prussia. After an uprising, Warsaw surrendered. In 1795, Prussia snatched Mazovia with Warsaw, Austria took the lands lying between the Pilica, Vistula, and Bug Rivers, and Russia took what was left. Poland was wiped off the map. Not until after World War I did Poland reappear on the map of Europe, after an absence of 123 years.

"In her moment of crisis, Poland could count on the sympathy of every state in Europe, and on the support of none."

—*Adam Zamoyski in* The Polish Way

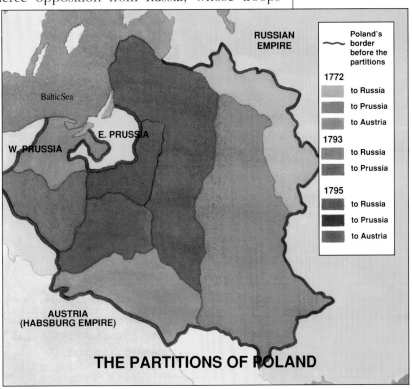

THE PARTITIONS OF POLAND

21

THE NEW NATION

During World War I, U.S. President Woodrow Wilson proclaimed that the complete restoration of a reunited, independent Poland was an incontrovertible aim of the Allies.

Independence was proclaimed on November 10, 1918 by Jozef Pilsudski, the founder of the Polish Legions fighting against Germany during the war. On June 28, 1919, the Treaty of Versailles officially recognized the independence of Poland although there was still more fighting to come. In 1920, the Red Army of Russia's new communist regime marched west toward Berlin, threatening Warsaw. The Polish army led by Pilsudski defended the city and launched a successful counterattack. Under the subsequent Peace of Riga, Poland's eastern border was fixed on the Zbrucz (shBRUHch) River.

Under the Second Polish Republic, a constitution was adopted in 1921 that established a parliament. Women were granted full rights. Years of instability followed, with 14 multi-party coalition governments holding power. Eventually, in 1926, Pilsudski seized power in a military coup and governed in an increasingly authoritarian manner until his death in 1935.

WORLD WAR II

Hitler wanted full German control over the "free city" of Gdansk, formerly called Danzig. He issued an ultimatum that Poland refused to accept, and World War II started. Warsaw was bombed by the Luftwaffe (German air force) at daybreak on September 1, 1939. On September 17, the Soviets invaded from the east. Although Great Britain and France had agreed to render military aid if Poland was attacked, no help arrived.

The spirited Polish army was defeated and Poland divided up between Nazi Germany and Soviet Russia in a fierce campaign lasting 36 days. Then

THE "FINAL SOLUTION"

The camps of Birkenau, Treblinka, and Majdanek were built by the Nazis for the specific purpose of destroying a nation of people. The "final solution" for Hitler turned Poland into a mass graveyard.

Previously a Polish military barracks, Auschwitz (right) was a labor concentration camp for Poles who were considered anti-Nazi. The cynical motto over the gate read *"Arbeit Macht Frei"* (Work Makes You Free). Only later was it turned into a death camp. On display today are piles of belongings (shoes, clothing, brushes, spectacles, baskets, suitcases) looted from those about to be murdered. There is a mountain of human hair and some of the material woven from it; and grey-blue tins of Zyklon-B, the poison used to kill the camp inmates.

Block 10 housed the women upon whom the Germans performed medical experiments aimed at preventing any more Jews being born. Block 11 was the prison within a prison. Minute, damp rooms in the basement were the punishment cells, too small for the prisoners to sit or even squat.

Birkenau (also called Auschwitz II) was built as a factory devoted to death. The gas chambers were disguised as a huge shower room. Some four million victims, mostly Polish Jews, were executed there. When mass graves began to cause problems—body gases escaped after a while and made cracks in the earth—the graves were dug up and the bodies burned instead. Ovens were built that could incinerate 4,756 bodies in 24 hours—six to eight train loads a day. Birkenau was almost totally destroyed by the Nazis who did not wish its grim secrets discovered.

began a reign of terror. Hitler wanted racial purity in his widening empire and Poles were regarded as a "sub-human" species. Anyone who was considered at odds with German policy was taken into "protective custody" in concentration camps. These became extermination camps. Russia depopulated their share of Poland. In one year almost two million Poles were deported in cattle trucks to Siberia or the Russian Arctic.

A Polish government-in-exile was formed in Paris and later moved to London. Within Poland, an underground Polish Home Army of about 500,000 people were busy destroying German communications, blowing up bridges, and hindering any production of war materials.

The Unknown Soldier's Tomb lies in Warsaw, a symbol of the thousands who died fighting for their country in World War II.

A COMMUNIST STATE

When Germany fell on May 8, 1945, Poland had lost over 6.5 million citizens, the capital was obliterated, and the people starving and impoverished. Europe's frontiers were redrawn. Poland lost 70,000 square miles to the Soviet Union but gained 39,000 square miles in the west from Germany. A "people's republic" was formed in which the party wielded all the power. Communist policy stated, "the land now belongs to the peasants."

Every major city except Cracow had to be rebuilt after the destruction of the war. But under Communist ideology, top priority was given to the building of steel, coal, iron, and armaments industries. Poland became a member of the Warsaw Pact—the Communist alliance. Everyday life under the Soviet regime became a nightmare. Children were encouraged to inform on their parents. People suspected of being hostile to the state were denounced, arrested, and executed without trial. The Roman Catholic Church was openly attacked, but the majority of people remained devoutly Catholic.

In efforts to win Polish support for the Soviet regime, free education and social security were promoted. Cheap books were published that were available to all. Food prices were subsidized. But the failure of the Soviet's six-year plan (1950–55) brought social discontent and increasing economic disaster. Workers in Poznan rioted with the slogan "No bread without freedom."

THE BEGINNING OF FREEDOM

"We possess nothing—except our past."

—a common Polish sentiment during Communist rule

October 19, 1956, was "That Famous Friday"—a showdown between Polish party leader Wladyslaw Gomulka and top Russian officials, including Soviet leader Nikita Khruschev. The only remaining Communist of importance still popular in Poland, Gomulka refused to be bullied into subservience to the Russian Communist hierarchy.

At 7 a.m. on that Friday, top Russian officials flew in to Warsaw and were taken to the Belvedere Palace. Soviet troops started to surround the city. Inside the palace, Gomulka was re-elected by the Central Committee. Messages of support from miners, steelworkers, and workers' unions were received by Gomulka, who needed all the help he could muster.

"We shall resort to force, since there is no other way to convince you!" shouted Khruschev. Gomulka retorted, "I am going in front of the microphone right now and I will tell the Polish people what you are demanding of us and what we are refusing to grant you." Tersely, he reminded the Russians of the economic collapse, the growing Polish resentment, the Russian economic exploitation, and the failure by Russia to repatriate some 500,000 Poles held captive since the war.

At 2 a.m. the next morning, the negotiations drew to a close. "Go to bed. We have won. The Russians are leaving," said a weary Gomulka when he reached his home. The Russian plane took off at 6:45 a.m. The people went wild. Cheering crowds filled the streets. Gomulka presented the nation with a virtual declaration of independence from the Soviet Union: "Poland has the right to be sovereign, and this sovereignty must be respected."

But by the summer, the economic crisis was so acute, the government could not maintain food subsidies. Price increases of 46% were proposed. Strikes and protests the next day were met by police brutality and arrests. About 2,000 people were detained, many savagely beaten in custody.

AFTER THE EXCITEMENT

"This is a powder keg, and it may blow up on us at any time, but Poland is where I belong."

— A Pole who returned in 1956

Gomulka had gained three concessions: an independent church, freedom from state-controlled agriculture, and some political freedom. But the new "Polish Communism" resulted in near starvation for much of the country. With the slogan "Bread and Liberty," the students rioted in 1968, there were shipyard strikes in 1970, and more strikes (particularly of factory workers) in 1975.

In July 1980, another attempt was made to raise food prices to a realistic level. Workers demanded wage increases to match, free trade unions, the reinstatement of dismissed workers, and the release of political prisoners. Their strike was a severe embarrassment to the government. Concessions reluctantly offered by the deputy prime minister were not agreed on by the Politburo. Instead, members of the Workers Defense Committee were detained and the editor of *Robotnik,* the magazine that linked workplaces around the country, was arrested and beaten up. By now most of the work force on the Baltic coast was on strike. In the subsequent meeting with government representatives, "Solidarity" was born.

SOLIDARITY LIVES!

Solidarity (Solidarnosc), swiftly growing to 10 million members, was the first free trade union in the Communist bloc. On December 13, 1981, General Wojciech Jaruzelski declared martial law. After operating openly for 16 months, the union was now banned. Six thousand of its leaders were arrested; hundreds were charged with treason and nine were killed. Solidarity leader Lech Walesa was locked up in a remote hunting lodge. Food shortages increased countrywide.

U.S. President Ronald Reagan and Pope John Paul II were convinced that if the Polish Communist government could be destabilized, it would

hasten the collapse of Soviet dominance in Eastern Europe. The key to this was Solidarity. Printing presses, computers, and shortwave radios were smuggled into Poland. The Vatican and the United States supported Solidarity with funds. The methods used were ingenious. At half time in a national soccer championship, a SOLIDARITY LIVES! banner appeared on the television screen and a message was broadcast calling for resistance. Communist control of the media had been beaten.

The Pope visited Poland in 1983, calling for conciliation. The Military Council was dissolved. The next year, 35,000 political prisoners were released on the 40th anniversary of the People's Republic.

In 1988, shipyards, mines, and steelworks were paralyzed by Solidarity-led strikes for higher wages after recent price rises. The government resigned, to be replaced by a new reformist, though still a Communist, administration. After weeks of Communist-Solidarity-Church negotiations, a historic accord was reached in April 1989. Solidarity was legally reinstated, opposition politics were to be tolerated, legal rights given to the Catholic Church, the state media monopoly lifted, and a new "socialist pluralist" Constitution adopted.

"This is Poland again; there is not the slightest doubt about it. We can talk, laugh, and grumble; we write whatever we please."

— *Zenon Poninski, a road engineer in Lowicz, quoted in* Home to Poland

LECH WALESA

Lech Walesa was born in 1943. At the age of 7, he started walking a daily mile to the village school, where he was a spirited student who loved to argue with his teachers. He hated farming and wanted to be an engineer. Although he passed his exams, his parents could not afford to send him to college. Discouraged, Walesa took a part-time job while attending courses at a trade school. During his military service, he was recom-mended for promotion, but Walesa did not choose to become a military leader.

Already known as a skilled worker, he found a job at the gigantic Lenin Shipyard in Gdansk. At work he laid electric cables in fishing boats; at home, in a cramped house shared with three other workers, Lech listened to Radio Free Europe and talked politics. He met Danuta Golos in a flower shop and a year later they were married.

The worsening Polish economy resulted in the shipyard workers being given less time to do a job, with no extra pay if the work took as long as before. Productivity did not increase and new price increases were announced just before Christmas 1970. Strikes erupted all along the Baltic coast. Lech Walesa was at the head of a column of protesters. From then on, his life was filled with speeches to his fellow workers and reasoned, if heated, arguments with his employers—and later with government representatives. When a worker with 30 years' service at the shipyard was fired in 1980 for distributing political pamphlets, the general indignation sparked off a strike demanding a free trade union, free speech, and the right to strike. Feeling strongly that God was on their side, Walesa negotiated a successful settlement and the Solidarity free trade union was born.

More years of political turmoil followed. Walesa (carried by supporters in the picture above) was spurned, praised, arrested, imprisoned—until in 1983 he was awarded the Nobel Peace Prize for his efforts. That brought added international prestige. He led the negotiations in 1989 that resulted in Poland's first non-Communist government in 40 years. By that time, Walesa with his wife and family lived in a large villa in Gdansk. Polish workers cheered him still, but saw that he was dressed better than they were, and getting a little fat and suffering from back trouble. He was tired and told them, "You have to create a couple of new Walesas. I did my part." But fate had yet another part in store for him. In December 1990, nine years after he and his movement had been banned, Lech Walesa became president of Poland.

THE IRON CURTAIN TORN ASIDE

Poland's first free elections in over 40 years were held in June 1989. Solidarity captured all but one of the Sejm and Senate seats they were entitled to contest. Czeslaw Kiszczak was asked to form a government but was unable to do so against the opposition of Solidarity, so he resigned. By September, a grand "coalition" had been formed with Tadeusz Mazowiecki as prime minister and Wojciech Jaruzelski as president. But the new government still faced the old economic problems: serious under-investment, poor industry, and limp productivity. Foreign investment was sought, a stock exchange opened, and the zloty (Polish currency) drastically devalued.

Mazowiecki resigned after a poor showing in the presidential elections in November 1990, in which Lech Walesa became president; the new government elected Jan Krzystof Bielecki as prime minister in January 1991. Poland's new political problem after years of one-party rule was that there were too many political parties, none of them strong enough to form a government without alliances with other parties. By January 1992 there was another prime minister: Jan Olszewski formed a new government "with a heavy heart and a true sense of responsibility."

Since 1989, there has been a relaxing of tight monetary controls in an effort to boost exports. The economy appears at last to be strengthening. In May 1992, Walesa, having lost confidence in the government, proposed the formation of a new cabinet. Successive ministers tried in vain to win sufficient support among the 17 different parties in the Sejm to form a strong base for governing. The coalition formed by Poland's first woman prime minister, Hanna Suchocka, was defeated in a no-confidence motion by one vote in May 1993. President Walesa dissolved Parliament and launched a "reform bloc" of his own.

A bank in Poland.

GOVERNMENT

IN TRUE MEDIEVAL TRADITION, government in Poland began with the nobility and the peasants. The "lord of the castle" made the laws and his peasants obeyed them. One such local leader formed the Piast dynasty that provided Poland's first kings. Power in Europe was a constant struggle between the state and the church. The Jagiellonian dynasty dominated the 15th and 16th centuries, during which Poland became more prosperous, and rich merchants joined the nobles as powers in the land.

In 1493, the Sejm was born, in which the Polish nobility sought to curb the powers of their king and of each other. The Sejm had agreed that all final decisions had to be unanimous. But officially, when it came to the vote, it only needed one man to veto (vote against) it, and the whole work of Parliament was cancelled out. That was the *Liberum veto*. Between 1696 and 1733, the Polish nobility agreed on so little that use of the veto became an epidemic.

THE FIRST CONSTITUTION

Officially Rzeczpospolita Polska ("RESH-pos-POL-ita POL-ska," Republic of Poland), Poland had the earliest constitution of any country in Europe. The anniversary of its adoption, on May 3, 1791, is an annual holiday. Only the United States has an earlier constitution—and by only four years! The Constitution introduced the concept of a people's sovereignty, including the middle classes as well as the nobility. Political and judicial power was separated. Government was delegated to a cabinet responsible to the Sejm. Cities were allowed self-determination, and the peasants gained legal protection. Unfortunately, well aware of the chaos and bloodshed caused in France by the people's revolution only two years before, neighboring Russia decided to protect the land it had already taken from Poland in 1772 by invading the rest. The Constitution was annulled.

Opposite: **Belvedere House, the residence of President Lech Walesa. It was the birthplace of democracy, where the "round table agreement" of 1989 was signed.**

REBIRTH OF DEMOCRACY

The rebirth of Polish democracy is forever enshrined in the "round table agreements" hammered out in 1989. Solidarity emerged victorious from the June elections and in September formed Poland's first non-Communist government since the late 1940s.

A 100-member Senate (upper house) was created with a power to veto Sejm decisions. The Sejm could only overrule this with a two-thirds majority vote. General Jaruzelski was elected president. The Communist nominee for prime minister, Czeslaw Kiszczak, failed to gather enough support to form a coalition government, so Solidarity put forward Tadeusz Mazowiecki, who was elected prime minister on August 24. But this was not the same Solidarity that had captured the imagination of the world in 1980–81. In those years, it represented the hopes of the Polish people. Now it triumphed largely because Poland refused to vote for the Communist Party.

Poles at the polls. The ballot box is red and white, the country's national colors. Poles call electioneering promises intended to attract votes *kielbasa wyborcza* or "election sausages!"

The year 1990 was the year Poland tried to change—some say too fast—from a totalitarian system to a pluralist democracy and a free market economy. The year ended with Lech Walesa as democratically elected president of the republic, but domestic politics had become more turbulent. During this time, food prices rose by up to 600%, a number of state monopolies were broken up, and unemployment reached 1.3 million. A new Constitution was being drafted. Censorship and the state mass media monopoly were ended. Registering a new political party became legal and easy. The security service was disbanded. In early 1991, the Sejm rejected President Walesa's proposed constitutional amendments. Voters eventually faced an election with 67 political parties. Of these, 29 parties won at least one seat—but over half of the people did not vote.

THE LAW

The Polish judicial system under Communist rule was headed by a supreme court appointed by the Council of State. All judges were appointed by the political leaders of the country. "Justice" went hand in hand with "politics"—and that meant the official Communist doctrine.

Polish policemen on crowd control duty in the capital.

That allegiance changed as soon as Communism died, but the legal system of a country cannot be changed so quickly. There is no jury system in Poland. Every case is heard by a judge and two "people's assessors," who are ordinary people elected by the local councils. There are two types of courts: the district court handles most cases, both civil and criminal, with serious cases being sent on to the county court. The supreme court in Warsaw is the chief judicial body in the country.

Polish law is based on the Constitution. This offers protection to the family as a unit, especially when children are involved. Simple cases, such as driving offenses and drunkenness, are dealt with by local misdemeanor boards made up of members elected from the local population. In the name of "reparation," land, houses, and goods confiscated by the Communist state are being returned to their rightful owners. The claims are countless.

GOVERNMENT TODAY

It was in Poland that the word "communist" was first used in 1569 to describe the way of life of the Polish Arians who believed in the common ownership of all material goods. Up to 40,000 converts were centered on Rakow, where their academy produced a fine translation of the Bible into Polish. Sadly, "communist" means something very different today.

In July 22, 1952, Poland became a "People's Republic" and since June 1989, the "Republic of Poland." Parliament consists of two chambers: the Sejm, with 460 deputies, each elected for four years; and the Senate, with 100 members. The president is the head of state, guardian of the republic's Constitution. He has the power to order parliamentary elections and to dissolve the Sejm and the Senate. The president is also the supreme commander of the armed forces of the republic.

The government is formed by the prime minister, who is nominated by the president and is usually the leader of the political party holding the most seats in the Sejm. Executive power is held by the cabinet, presided over by the prime minister.

The Sejm, like most parliaments, passes bills, adopts the state budget and economic plan, and appoints the 24-member executive council of ministers (cabinet) headed by the prime minister. When Poland was under Soviet control, 55% (253) of the Sejm's seats were reserved for candidates from the Patriotic Movement for National Rebirth (PRON), which was the broad front organization for the Communist Party. Today, there are 12 political parties with representatives freely elected; none holds more than 62 seats (14%).

The Senate is the upper chamber of the National Assembly. Its role in the new political system has not been clearly defined by the Constitution, but in practice the Senate acts as a mouthpiece for local government and for observance of citizens' rights and freedoms.

As recently as May 1993, Poland seemed unable to find political stability. Prime Minister Hanna Suchocka's reformist minority government suffered a vote of no-confidence, but President Lech Walesa refused to accept her resignation and instead disbanded the parliament. He has launched the BBWR (Movement for Helping Reform), which he hopes politicians will join on a non-party basis, and has signed into law new rules to help limit the number of parties represented in the parliament.

Four years after Poland turned its back on Communism, the majority of Poles are disappointed with the political situation. More than 20 political parties have made it impossible to form a stable government, unemployment runs at 14%, and living standards are falling once more.

Nie damy sie (We will not give in) has been the slogan of Polish leaders for 200 years. So it is not surprising that a parliament with so many political parties has found it difficult to form a coalition strong enough to govern. Yet Poland was making progress. The transition to democracy argued out in that "round table agreement" between the Communists and Solidarity in 1989 set out clearly what each side could expect from the other. Today, Poland is experiencing a slow but sure revival of its economy. By contrast, Russia and its former partners in the Soviet Union are in political and economic turmoil.

A man begs on the street in Warsaw.

REGIONAL ADMINISTRATION

Local government is allocated first to the 49 *voivodships* (provinces), including three cities with that status (Warsaw, Cracow, Lodz) that have their own elected people's councils. Within those areas, the local population of each *gmina* (ward) is encouraged to set up self-governing "commonwealths." In 1992, there were 2,459 such People's Communal Councils in Poland, elected for a period of four years.

It was admitted in 1990 that the communal council elections of June 1988 had been undemocratic, and new elections were held on May 27 for 2,348 councils.

ECONOMY

POLAND IS THE FIRST COUNTRY freed from Communism to see its economy expand—perhaps only 3 or 4%, but that is good news. Poland's economic revival was supported by the International Monetary Fund, which granted a one-year loan of $655 million.

TURNING POINT

Shock therapy to the Polish economy began in January 1990 when a 22% collapse of industrial output reduced the country's economy by 12%, followed by a further 7.5% in 1991. The turning point came with a slight growth in 1992.

After three years of economic upheaval, Poland is beginning to compete in world markets. Yet this optimism has not reached Poles concerned with the daily business of survival. The beggars on the streets of Warsaw are a constant reminder that many still live in poverty. Peasant farmers have seen their income drop by 50% over the past five years. Unemployment is rising toward three million people (16% of the labor force).

An economy changing from Communist-minded state monopolies to privatized companies in an open market is bound to suffer birth pangs. Basic industries such as shipbuilding and coal mining still need restructuring. Obsolete industries have to phased out. Even the trade union leaders who fought against the power of Communism are obsolete in an economic climate where "small is beautiful" and private enterprise is taking over from corporate power.

Opposite: **Poland's economy is turning around. It is now a country of great opportunity for private enterprise, such as this McDonald's fast-food outlet.**

Below: **Bricklayers in a church courtyard. Poles are very concerned with the daily business of survival.**

AT THE BANK

Polish banknotes tell their own story. The smaller denominations are dated 1982—before the collapse of Communism. Higher denominations of 100,000, 500,000, or one million zloty or more are dated 1988. Such huge sums were not needed until free market inflation arrived. It is not difficult to be a millionaire in Poland!

The 1,000 zloty banknote in the picture (right) has a portrait of Mikolaj Kopernik, a Polish astronomer, while the 5,000 zloty banknote has a portrait of Frederic Chopin, the famous composer. Some other famous people featured on Polish banknotes are Ignacy Jan Paderewski, a pianist and politician who was prime minister of Poland in 1919, on the 2,000,000 zloty banknote; Wladyslaw Reymont, a Polish writer awarded a Nobel Prize in Literature, on the 1,000,000 zloty banknote; Henryk Sienkiewicz, another Nobel Prize winner in Literature and the author of *Quo Vadis*, on the 500,000 zloty banknote; and Marie Curie, Nobel Prize winner in the field of physics and chemistry, on the 20,000 zloty banknote.

A FARMING COUNTRY

Poland is still a largely farming country, Eastern Europe's largest producer of agricultural crops after what was the Soviet Union, with about 10 million farms employing nearly a third of its total population. Arable crops such as wheat, rye, potatoes, sugar beet, and fruit form over half the output, alongside livestock production of cattle and sheep and about 20 million pigs. For many years Poland exported agricultural produce, but a series of bad harvests after 1975 led to imports of fodder and grain.

For a country so long under Soviet domination, Poland is unusual in having over three-quarters of its farmland privately owned. The Poles hated working on a farm that did not belong to their own family, so production on state farms and cooperatives dropped disastrously. Most of the farms are small, often with inherited strips of land widely separated, and without the previous Communist state subsidies on materials and fuel, many farms are economically unsound. Modern machinery is used where it can be afforded, but there are about two million draft horses still at work.

A coal-fired power station in Poland.

COAL IS A MAJOR EXPORT

There has been mining in Poland since medieval times—chiefly coal (hard coal and brown coal) as well as sulfur, copper, lead, and zinc. Coal is Poland's major export (in 1991, over 20 million tons) and the country is the fourth largest coal supplier in the world. Other industries produce steel, chemicals, household glass, paper, washing machines, refrigerators, televisions, and motor vehicles. When many of the industrial areas were set up, more than 50% of the exports went to the Soviet Union or other Communist countries because the bulk of industry was state-owned. Now most exports go to the European Community countries.

Another major industry is shipbuilding. Many of the shipyards were destroyed in World War II, and it was not until 1949 that the first postwar ocean-going vessel was launched. Under state control there was swift progress, with Poland changing from steamships to diesel. In the 1970s the yards were modified with new technology. The Lenin Shipyard in Gdansk could boast of a steady output of factory ships for fishing fleets, ferries, container ships, and bulk cargo carriers.

Industrial pollution has done a lot of damage in Poland. Now steps are being taken to prevent any increase, while ecological cleaning up is emphasized at existing works and factories. Plans to build an iron ore mine and an ironworks in the Suwalki region, an aluminum oxide plant near Kielce, and a lignite (brown coal) mine near Poznan have been stopped because they would have endangered the environment.

During the long years of Communist rule, Poles had to stand in long lines to buy most of their basic needs.

SHOPPING

During the 40 years of Communist control, Polish men and women stood in long lines for the most basic foodstuffs or for clothes. Shopping could be an all-day occupation. The expression *niema* (NY-e-ma), which means "there is none," became almost a joke. Now all the goods they could want are in the shops, but not everyone can afford to buy them. During the economic crisis years of 1990–91, the income of worker families in the towns dropped by 25% and that of the rural farmers by 45%. Today, family incomes in Poland are still sadly low.

Meanwhile, during 1992, prices of consumer goods rose by 40%, so most housewives spent time comparing prices before buying anything. Most traveled by bus, and the favorite topic of conversation was where the best bargain could be found. Food took up 45% of the weekly paycheck, followed by about 10% on clothes. The average monthly wage was around $280; in 1991 it was below $150. In the first excitement of seeing shop shelves full, Poles bought things merely because goods were available. It was estimated that every Pole has five pairs of jeans! About 40% of Polish families own a car—usually a small Polish vehicle. The great dream is to have a telephone. For so many years, the waiting list for telephones was endless.

Every Saturday afternoon, a local bazaar arrives in front of the three huge department store buildings in Warsaw, under the shadow of the Palace of Culture and Science. Hundreds of Poles bring goods for sale, probably obtained during weekend trips to Berlin, which is very close to the western border of Poland, or visits farther abroad. Spread out on car hoods or just on the sidewalks are clothes, watches, radios, and micro-chip gadgets. This is a vital way of bringing extra income to the family budget. Most of these goods come from a carefully planned trading expedition that managed to avoid customs and import duties.

Whether this is smuggling or "trade tourism" depends on your point of view. It is now on the decline, but it still exists. The Poles are independent in their thinking and see rules as a challenge to their ingenuity. Allowed access to West Berlin in 1989, they flooded in with vodka at half the usual price, found ready customers, and loaded up with suitable goods to sell back home.

An unofficial "Polish market" forms as women sell goods on the steps of the subway.

TRADE UNIONS

Under Communist rule, efficiency was not considered as important as full employment. But what mattered to the Polish people was a wage sufficient to feed their families. So the slogan "Good Bread for Good Work" was coined in 1980 when the government attempted to raise food prices drastically without raising wages.

SOLIDARITY

In December 1970, workers were killed in front of the gates of the Lenin Shipyard in Gdansk when they wanted to protest about price increases. Ten thousand marchers had to be stopped by tanks sent by the Politburo. In 1980, in the same place, the 37-year-old Lech Walesa was elected chairman of a new labor union independent of the state. It was called Solidarity. It was not the first: a free trade union had been founded in Silesia in February 1978, and the Free Trade Union of the Coast was founded at Gdansk in April 1978.

Solidarity soon changed into a political movement. Eleven citizen committees were formed to represent the opposition to Communist rule, and in the elections of June 1989, Tadeusz Mazowiecki (editor-in-chief of the Solidarity newspaper) headed the first freely elected non-Communist government within the Warsaw Pact of Communist-controlled countries. The success story of Solidarity inspired similar "people power" movements in other East European countries.

THE SOVIET LEGACY

The industrial projects so energetically started during Communist rule were either wrongly sited, like the Katowice steel complex in Silesia, supplied with ore from the Soviet Union 1,250 miles away, or uneconomic because of an oversupply in the world steel market. Debts mounted. Poland could not repay what it had borrowed because it could not sell its products to the West. In desperation, scarce foodstuffs, raw materials, and fuel were sold abroad, which caused acute shortages at home. When a state of emergency was declared in 1980, Poland suspended the repayment of foreign loans. This led to a foreign debt of $43,000 million by 1990.

The trouble was that, to earn enough to support a family, it was almost impossible to be honest. So workers in factories stole wagon-loads of coal, clerks in state shops stole merchandise and resold it, tax collectors accepted bribes to keep quiet. A Communist deputy once calculated that about $120,000 was handed out in bribes every day, and just under a million dollars' worth of merchandise was stolen each day. Poles became accustomed to shrugging off any qualms at "cheating the government."

Opposite, top picture: **General Jaruzelski (second from right) with Warsaw Pact leaders. The general proclaimed martial law in December 1981. Solidarity was declared illegal.**

Opposite, box picture: **A poster declares General Jaruzelski a wanted man.**

43

BOOKS FOR PULP

Skladnica Ksiegarska, the state-owned wholesale book monopoly, is now bankrupt, owing $13 million. Its only assets are 12 million books. If they are sold off cheaply, they will flood the market and threaten Poland's 1,000 private publishers. If the company is liquidated, what about supplies of books to the rural areas where the booksellers do not want to trade? The books could be pulped—but there are 4,000 tons of them!

PROBLEMS OF A FREED MARKET

"We, too, will one day be efficient. But we have to fire all our planners first."

—an old Polish saying

In 1989, the year of political reform, inflation was running at over 600%. Wide-ranging measures to convert the economy into a market-oriented system were passed. Price subsidies were abolished, foreign investment encouraged, and state enterprises were turned into private ownership through the issue of "privatization bonds" and the shares sold readily. The zloty was substantially devalued.

Swiftly, industry declined by 30%, sales of locally produced goods by 37%, and real wages by 33%. By the end of 1990, the recession had slowed, but real income remained 30% below the 1989 level. Whereas in the Communist era, unemployment had been officially stated as zero, it now stood at 1.3 million: 8% of the workforce. The World Bank approved loans of $900 million to boost exports and natural gas production and to build up a market economy.

In 1991, the second year of "economic shock therapy," Poland was faced with a huge hard currency debt. Borrowings had reached $48.5 billion. In March, the "Paris Club" of 17 European nations that had loaned money to Poland wrote off half Poland's debt, provided Poland kept to a program to stabilize its economy set by the International Monetary Fund. Five days later, the United States promised to cut Poland's debts by 70%; Germany and France had already made similar reductions in support of Poland's change to democracy. Poland, in return, undertook to cut government spending by a third. Harsh cuts were made to social projects and welfare benefits. Output fell by a further 3% (after a 13% fall in 1990), and the previous year's 550% inflation was reduced to 60–80%.

THE MARKET PLACE OF TOMORROW

Poland presents a great opportunity for private enterprise. Foreign firms such as Fiat, Coca Cola, and Unilever are starting to invest. Eighty important French firms, including four of the largest banks, have branch offices in Warsaw. Large American corporations are buying shares in Polish construction and telecommunications companies.

Entrepreneurs are grabbing at the tax advantages offered by trading as wholesalers: the sign *Hurtownia* (wholesale) is seen everywhere. The Warsaw Stock Exchange opened in April 1991. Within a year it had transacted $80 million worth of business. The income tax system is reportedly "clogged." VAT (value-added tax) is due to arrive soon.

Computer firms such as IBM (from the United States) and TBT (from Japan) have opened branches in Poland. "As far as computer equipment is concerned, it is clear that Poland will never outdistance Japan, but in software the Poles are better than the Japanese," says Wieslaw Romanowski, a Pole who has lived in Japan for 16 years and who owns a Tokyo computer company.

With the collapse of Communism, the Iron Curtain seemed to be torn apart. But for Poland to be welcomed into European trading circles will be harder. Europe's subsidized steelmakers, for example, already produce more than they need, so Polish steel is not welcomed. Perhaps as many as 70,000 jobs will be lost in Poland as the steel mills adjust to more realistic production targets, cutting output in 1993 to about half the 1990 level. The European Community has welcomed Poland as a new democracy, but not yet as an equal trading partner.

Foreign firms see Poland as the place to invest. This Athlete's Foot store in Cracow is an American franchise selling sports goods.

POLISH PEOPLE

THE WORD POLANI means "people of the fields." That was their name long before modern industry had brought in mechanized agriculture. Scythes and horse-drawn ploughs are still in use.

Poland today is the most homogeneous state in Europe—meaning that the Poles are from one original race of people. They are almost all Slavs, they speak the same language with some regional differences, and almost all are Roman Catholics. Due to their Slavic characteristics, Poles are generally blonder and have lighter-colored eyes than the peoples of southern Europe, but are darker than the Scandinavians. With successive invasions and inevitable inter-marriages, the blond hair that had formerly distinguished the Slavs changed in some individuals to the darker hair of the typical mid-European of today. Most Poles and Czechoslovaks are Slavs, and they form about a quarter of the Slav population of the world. The Polish population of 38.3 million is a young one—the average age is 29—making Poland the nation with the youngest population in Europe after Albania.

Poland's borders have shifted widely through the centuries, so the present country of Poland contains some minority groups, which include Germans, Ukrainians, and Belorussians. Many Poles have chosen or been forced to live in exile. During World War II, the Soviets sent thousands to Kazakhstan in Central Asia where they were forbidden to speak Polish or say anything about what had happened to them. Many are still there.

Poles can claim success in good looks: Aneta Kreglicka, a fair-haired beauty, was Miss Poland and Miss World in 1989.

Opposite: **An elderly woman stands at the doorway of her home in the mountains.**

STATISTICS

Age distribution:		Population:	Life expectancy:	
0–16	29%	density: 313 persons	men	66.5 years
17–59	57%	per square mile	women	75.5 years
60+	13%	urban population: 60%		

MINORITY GROUPS

The traditional Polish dress is popular during festivals and among little girls in Poland.

Marauding Magyar horsemen swept through Poland in the 9th century; Mongol horsemen invaded in the 13th century. The Polish king subsequently opened his country to outsiders, if they would come and repopulate its devastated lands. Millions came, including Jews fleeing persecution. Poland in the 15th and 16th centuries was a country of religious toleration. There were synagogues in most Polish towns and nearly 100 mosques as well. Constantly shifting borders through the centuries have resulted in small pockets of ethnic minorities being left inside or outside Poland. When the borders of the Second Republic were drawn in 1919–21, Poland was the sixth largest territory in Europe. Its ethnic minorities totalled some 9 million— about a third of the population.

UKRAINIANS When the borders were changed yet again in 1945, there were some 700,000 Ukrainians living in Poland. Some moved reluctantly to what became the Ukrainian Socialist Soviet Republic. Most preferred to stay where they were and fought for the right to do so. By 1947, Polish authorities decided to distribute the remaining 200,000 Ukrainians elsewhere. Most were sent to the west, where there were farms left empty by the departed

Germans, but no more than two or three Ukrainian families were ever allowed to settle in the same village. Deliberately split apart, some 300,000 Ukrainians today struggle to maintain their own traditions. Only one primary school and two high schools offer Ukrainian language courses. Although many of their churches have fallen into disrepair, efforts are now being made to conserve them. The Festival of Ukrainian Culture at Sopot, where choirs and dance groups celebrate with true Ukrainian music, is held only once every two years.

BELORUSSIANS In the east of Poland are some 170,000 Belorussians, mostly concentrated around the Bialystok area. A Belorussian Democratic Union was founded in 1990 to represent their interests. Near Siemiatycze is the Holy Mount of Grabarka. At the festival of Corpus Christi, the Belorussian pilgrims who belong to the old Orthodox Church climb to the summit carrying crosses.

LITHUANIANS About 10,000 Lithuanians live near the border with Lithuania. They have their own primary and high school in Punsk. There is also a Lithuanian Social and Cultural Society.

GERMANS The German minority is concentrated in the industrial region of south and southwestern Poland known as Silesia. The Potsdam Conference of 1945 approved the repatriation of Germans, who were replaced by Poles returning home from exile or imprisonment in the Soviet Union and other countries. So the people in the west and southwest are not all descended from original Polish inhabitants. In fact, many are of pure German ancestry. In the 1980s, as the economic crisis in Poland increased, many German-speaking Silesians remembered their ethnic ties with West Germany and considered emigration.

"Poland is our homeland, but it does not belong only to Poles. We share this country with people of other nationalities."

—Tadeusz Mazowiecki, in his inaugural speech as prime minister, September 1989

POLISH JEWS

The first Jews to settle in Poland probably came from beyond the Volga River, an area that had established Judaism as a state religion in the 8th century. When Jews were expelled from other European countries in the Middle Ages, they were always accepted in Poland. They were allowed to develop their own culture and customs. In 1939 there were about 3.5 million Jews in Poland—about 10% of the country's population. Doctors, teachers, scientists, industrialists, bankers, and businessmen—they were accepted by all. The meat trade was virtually run by them.

Most Polish Jews, especially the lower classes who were tailors and cobblers, were Orthodox Jews and vehemently anti-Communist. More important, they wanted to be left alone. So the violence of the Nazi occupation, during which almost the entire Jewish population was deliberately exterminated, remains a horrific chapter in Polish history.

A Jewish cemetery in Warsaw.

There are Jewish families still, mostly in the urban areas, a tiny remnant of the former three million. These people are Poles in all except language. Perhaps no more than 5,000 in all, the Jews maintain their own organizations and schools. They run a Jewish theater and in Warsaw there is a Jewish Historical Institute with its own library and museum.

THE GORALE

The Polish highlanders are an independent-minded people with their own mountain way of life. The Gorale (gor-ARL) live in the southwest region known as the Podhale. They are traditionally pastoralists, raising sheep and goats, cultivating only a few crops of oats, barley, or potatoes. Today, with more modern agricultural methods available, they have ventured into dairy farming. Division of labor is based on age and gender. For men, the work involves horses, machinery, and tools such as scythes. Women and children rake, turn hay, plant and gather potatoes, and weed the vegetables.

Most Gorale live in small villages—clusters of wooden houses surrounded by long strip fields, pastures, and forest. Although there is a growing tendency for young couples to establish a new household, the three-generation extended family is still common. Old two-room wooden huts stand beside modern multi-story brick houses. But even in modern houses, the family tends to live, eat, and sleep in one or two rooms, while renting the other rooms to tourists.

The Podhale has several market towns and a few resorts. One of the poorest areas in Poland, it is now benefiting from the tourist dollar.

The Gorale are strongly and uniformly Catholic. For them, religious events are the most important yearly events. Every Easter, Christmas, and May (the month the Virgin Mary's ascent into heaven is celebrated) the churches and roadside shrines are beautifully decorated.

The old lifestyle has been maintained despite years under Austrian rule, occupation by Nazi forces, and the Communist state. The people have succeeded in keeping a reputation for interfamily and intervillage blood feuds, and generally rebellious behavior.

Loggers at work in the Tatra mountains. The highlanders are an independent-minded people who maintain their mountain way of life.

TRADITIONAL COSTUMES

Back in the 14th century, only the nobility had the right to wear red. The word *karmazyn* (crimson) came to mean "gentleman" as well. Today, Poles often wear clothes of predominantly red and white because those are the national colors of Poland.

The *kontousch* overgarment with slashed sleeves and its *joupane* undergarment of a long tunic both show the influence of the Asiatic world. The style was probably copied from Persia, for Poland used to stretch as far as the Black Sea. Similarly, the baggy pants and flowing cloaks of the men could well have Turkish origins. They wore fur caps over their short cropped hair or long locks. These were clothes for rich folk: peasants wore short tunics of handwoven materials in soft natural colors, long pants, a cloak of sheepskin, and boots or shoes made from woven strips of bark.

The important element is decoration: edgings in brightly contrasting materials, trimmings of colored strings, red or green lapels on coats,

TATRA FINERY

For the Gorale of the Tatra Mountains, religious events are very important. People put on traditional costumes to attend mass and join in processions round the church. Lace-trimmed aprons are flaunted over colorful skirts with embroidered "waistcoat" tops, and black, gold-trimmed caps adorn women's heads. The men wear white felt pants with a striped design at the side, broad belts, sometimes sashes, and black brimmed hats. The shepherds carry traditional ax-like crooks, which are practical items much needed when rescuing a stray lamb from a mountainside.

studded belts, metal ornaments, appliqué work, and embroidery. The richest appliqué work can be seen on the leather bodices and pants in the Carpathian mountain area. Lace and crochet work are made in intricate designs, especially in Silesia.

Polish women delight in wearing an amber bead necklace. This was a way for a prospective bride to show off her wealth. Amber from the Baltic is increasingly precious, especially if there is a fossilized insect trapped in the resin. Coral beads are thought to bring good luck in the shape of many healthy children!

Nowadays, such finery is reserved for Sunday dress or special religious festivals. On those days, women wear bright-colored pleated skirts, red and blue, with a richly floral blouse and a headscarf for the older ones. For the rest of the week, they wear more somber garb: black skirts and dark suits in the towns; otherwise jeans, like anywhere else.

Another part of Polish tradition is their love of horses. Horses were a symbol of warrior status. They were lovingly cared for, covered in rich cloths when on parade, adorned with plumes, and even dyed on special occasions. The favorite color was red, but for funerals black with a purple or green mane and tail was a popular combination. The Poles crossed Turkish horses with European breeds, and in the 17th century, Polish cavalry outnumbered the infantry by three to one.

Opposite: **The baggy pants of these folk musicians suggest a Turkish influence.**

Below: **Amber from the Baltic is much prized.**

LIFESTYLE

"I MAY BE THE HEAD of the family, but I believe the mother is the heart," says the true Polish father. Although in modern families both husband and wife go out to work, men still believe that a mother should be at home. This belief is particularly strong in Silesia, where they object strongly to husband and wife being taxed separately. The idea of "family" remains important in both town and country, and the sacrifices parents still make for their children are even stronger. This emphasis on the family unit was strengthened during the brutal years of martial law which ended in 1983. There were random searches on the streets, and with many unsuspected government informers, no one knew whom to trust any more. So people withdrew into their immediate family circle.

Now that the four and a half decades of repressive totalitarianism in Poland have ended, the feeling is not that of "liberation," but of venturing into an unknown freedom.

Opposite: **Picnicking by a mountain stream. Polish families look forward to enjoying weekends in the country.**

Left: **A family feeds the birds in the town square. The family is important whether one lives in the town or the country.**

A PATRIOTIC PEOPLE

It is difficult, if not dangerous, to attempt to sum up national characteristics, but robust patriotism is surely the keynote to Polish character. Few could deny that the Poles have been determined and cheerful in the face of hardship. This has resulted in a rowdy, friendly public life. During martial law when protest could bring imprisonment, many Poles wore buttons that said, in large letters, "DOWN WITH THE MILITARY JUNTA" and, in very tiny letters, "in El Salvador." An insignificant protest, but typical of the Polish refusal to admit defeat. After the secret police were removed in October 1956, freedom of speech became a Polish delight. In the crowded cafés, Poles can talk out loud instead of whispering.

The Palace of Culture and Science, a gift from Stalin to the Polish people.

The wry Polish humor is well illustrated in the way that local citizens will explain to visitors that the best point from which to admire Warsaw is from the top of the 37-story Palace of Culture and Science. Why? Because it is the only place from which you can't see the Palace of Culture and Science! This "wedding-cake skyscraper" was a gift from Soviet leader Joseph Stalin and is thoroughly disliked by Poles as a symbol of Soviet domination.

Rejoicing in their new-born democracy, Poles often disguise their present struggles for jobs, for money, or for the things their children need with stories of past horrors. They remind each other how it used to take eight weeks to get the application form for a passport and a year for a television set, how they were allocated a number on a waiting list, and had to pay a bribe simply to keep their place on that list.

Another touch of Polish optimism is their insistence that it never rains on Saturdays. "Saturday is the day the Blessed Virgin does the celestial washing. Therefore it cannot rain."

During the war years, the workers at a steel mill altered the dimensions on the working drawings for all the conning-towers they produced for German submarines so that they failed to fit onto the hulls. Teams of investigators failed to find out the cause, so production ceased. Blame was put on the inefficiency of the Polish workers whereas, in fact, they had been skilled and efficient enough to hide what was going on!

AN ECCENTRIC POLE

Poles are fond of their eccentricity. They tell the story of Karol Radziwill, an eccentric 18th century Polish nobleman more fond of drinking than most. His favorite activity was apparently shooting at flying bison, which were catapulted into the air for the purpose. In his Christian chapel, music was provided by a Jewish orchestra dressed as Turkish soldiers. When criticized that he lived better than the king, Radziwill said, "I live like a Radziwill—the king can live how he likes."

POVERTY-LINE LIVING

The Polish economy is improving at last, but that still means hard times for most ordinary families. Ever since martial law, Poles have not trusted the banks, fearing that accounts might be frozen. So for years their money, especially any U.S. dollars or Deutschemarks, was hidden in mattresses or in socks stuffed up chimneys!

Sunday market in Warsaw where stalls sell anything and everything.

In those bitter times past, you had to be a member of the ruling party to live in more than one room. Nowadays, apartments are still just as hard to find, but there is no regime to blame it on. Children may sleep in bunk beds in the one-room family home. A communal kitchen and a bathroom may be shared by five families. Nobody moves much, for fear of losing a job or an apartment, or both.

In a desire to forget economic troubles, millions of gallons of alcoholic drinks, mostly beer and vodka, are consumed, but both government and church are trying to help the people deal with the problem of alcoholism.

The days of "black market" shops supplementing the state network are over. There are no longer empty shelves or lines for scarce items. Shops have almost everything anyone could want—provided they can afford it. Most cannot. So women sell produce or flowers on the street corner. Houses in the country are made of bare concrete blocks and a few unplastered bricks.

CHILDREN

A street in Warsaw is called Kubus Puhatek—or Winnie-the-Pooh—named at the request of Polish children. What other country would take their children so seriously?

Polish children grow up with mops of straight dark hair or unruly fair hair and often intense blue eyes. They are delicately featured—a curious contrast to Polish adults, many of whom have solid bodies and hard-boned faces. In between lie the years of work and worry. For country children, the one common ambition is to go to the city. Originally, this was in search of work, but it may now be more in search of the modern entertainments not available in rural life.

Polish children are polite. Some are still taught to click their heels smartly and kiss a woman's hand. Given an opportunity, they will shower a visitor with questions about "life in the West." They dress brightly in jeans or trousers, sweatshirts or a shirt with a loose jacket, and sneakers of all colors. Imitation military camouflage pants are popular. There are no school uniforms.

School hours have been reduced, and this means that many children leave school before their parents are home from work. There is a growing unease at the number who wander the streets with nothing worthwhile to do—and video rentals are rising to help these children pass the time.

The age of maturity in Poland is 18. Only then does the "child" gain full rights of Polish citizenship.

A group of school children visit Wawel Palace in Cracow. Poles have a saying that a child drinks the love of Poland with its mother's milk.

EDUCATION

Poles value education and knowledge highly. As early as 1773, a national education commission was established. This was the first central non-religious education authority in Central Europe. The system this commission established, of elementary school, high school, and college education, has lasted until today, the only addition being the recent one of nursery school.

School—from nursery through high school—is compulsory and free between the ages of 7 to 17. High schools can be grammar, art, technical, agricultural, or professional. The system is standard throughout the country, and Polish culture and history are strongly emphasized. Just over one million pupils attend 12,000 nursery schools; over five million pupils under 90,000 teachers attend 18,000 junior schools; and over two million pupils attend 6,000 secondary schools. Poland claims 98% literacy for its population, with a 97% attendance at school.

In high school, students usually specialize. Subject choices include biology, chemistry, mathematics, German, and English. Lessons last from 8 a.m. to 1 p.m. or 2:30 p.m. at the latest, and there's lots of homework! There is a new emphasis on the teaching of foreign languages and on computer skills. The number of pupils in high schools has increased, so there could be more undergraduates in Polish colleges within the next few years. Poland boasts a total of 90 colleges, academies, and

Children in junior school.

Jagiellonian University in Cracow, built in the 14th century. Copernicus studied there.

other schools. But at present there are only a limited number of actual college places. There are some dormitories for students; the others find rented rooms.

Poland is proud of its colleges. The Jagiellonian University in Cracow was founded in 1364; in Central Europe, only the University of Prague is older. In the 1980s, students studied with teachers banned from teaching by attending classes that moved from one apartment to another. These became known as Flying Universities. There is a crowded college in Warsaw as well that has achieved a curious fame because its library, for lack of space, shelves books by size instead of by subject.

As with so much of modern Poland, education is suffering from the need to be "cost effective." Teachers accustomed to believing they had a job for life were outraged at the suggestion that they could be fired if they did not produce results. Economies have resulted in fewer teaching hours, and in some schools, there is a double shift—some pupils attend school in the morning, and others in the afternoon for maximum classroom use.

Tightened budgets mean that some optional classes have been discontinued. Schools have to find sponsors or engage in fund-raising activities to bring in extra income.

STATE OF HEALTH

The Polish socialist state used to assure its citizens of full medical care at no cost. But this, like the bland assertion of full employment, was only propaganda. The general health of the country was low, and medical standards were poor. Poles went to a pharmacy if they felt ill and consulted the pharmacist there. They were reluctant to go to a hospital where there were too many patients for the beds, a lack of medicines, and sometimes unsanitary conditions.

Even today, doctors have a heavy workload and private treatment is expensive. There is a social health service run by the central Ministry of Health and Social Care. This includes clinics, hospitals, sanatoriums, ambulance services, and national sanitary inspection. There is one hospital bed for every 144 people and one doctor for every 480.

Social insurance covers free treatment for all workers and their families, as well as pensioners, invalids, and students. There are a few hundred homes for social care, catering for pensioners, the chronically sick, and the mentally retarded.

FLOWER SELLERS EVERYWHERE!

Poles love flowers. They grow them in flower beds, window boxes, and on balconies. Their traditional dress designs, pottery, and woodcarvings are all flower-decked. Poppies and roses predominate, with cornflowers, marigolds, or blue and purple crocuses in the springtime. It is a Polish custom to bring flowers when visiting—for a birthday, nameday, wedding, Sunday lunch, anything! So there are flower-sellers everywhere, and flower shops are open on Sundays. Bouquets of roses or carnations resplendent in a silver paper sheath are popular. A Polish cemetery is bright with flowers, too. After so many wars, such places are important to the Poles. In few other countries have the living so many dead to honor.

SPECIAL SUNDAY

"Six days shalt thou labor," says the Biblical commandment. In Poland, survival is a family commitment, especially in the country. Children work in the fields on Saturdays or during school holidays, turning hay or tending animals.

On leisurely Sunday, Poles love to walk about town, ride a bike, walk in the park, or engage in a dozen other relaxing pursuits.

But Sunday is different. For a rural family, the day may start with a bath for all. Then father puts on his Sunday suit and polished pointed shoes. Mother is perhaps showing off her traditional dress with its floral patterns and bright bodice. The children are smart in clean jeans and a freshly ironed shirt with a bright scarf. The house is tidied and the chores done, and off they go to the 11 o'clock mass.

When the service is over, it's time to gossip. There may be stalls set up in the churchyard, with flowers or local produce. Poles don't miss the chance for a sale! The men gather for a drink; boys and girls take the opportunity to chat; but the women hurry back to prepare the Sunday lunch. The long afternoon is a parade down the central street. Couples stroll hand in hand, eating ice-cream. Youths race their bikes through the park. Some Poles just lean out from their apartment balconies and share the evening sun with their friends.

ON THE MOVE

Traffic tends to move at a leisurely rate in Poland. There are still no completed expressways, but there are sections of *autobahn* (highways) inherited from Germany. Almost 4,000 miles of local roads and 1,300 miles of highways are being planned at a total estimated cost of $4.5 billion.

Driving has not adapted to the late 20th century. On weekdays, motorcycles, bicycles, tractors, and horsecarts happily join the "main" road to town. There are still cobbled lanes in some areas. Village pedestrians think the roads belong to them, especially after a party! In towns, jaywalkers can be fined on the spot.

The car seen everywhere is the 650 cc Fiat, the cheapest vehicle available and known as the "Polish Porsch." Toyota, Ford, and Peugeot are there as well. Parking space is in short supply, so most people park on the sidewalks.

City traffic—a mixture of trams, buses, and cars.

Polish families like to go visiting. Not many villagers have cars, so trains and buses are very important. The Polish State Railway trains are among the busiest in Europe. All large cities have commuter trains that are crowded. Buses are cheaper, but these too are usually crowded.

There are 2,500 miles of navigable rivers and canals. Poland's international airports are at Warsaw, Cracow, Katowice, and Gdansk, and there are eight other airports for domestic flights.

COUNTRY LIFE

On the Polish plains, peasants have cultivated wheat, rye, and vegetables for centuries. Through the rise and fall of great empires that brought maurading armies, it was the noble houses and great castles that tended to be destroyed. As the smoke cleared, the farmers returned to work. Communists, like previous invaders, drove out the landowners, but the farmer and the priest remained. Indeed, the clergy is present at every important social event: mainly christenings, weddings, and funerals.

Land ownership consists mainly of scattered small strips, as it was in the Middle Ages. This is the result of a complicated system of private ownership in which land was divided among a man's heirs. People who married someone from another village could end up with land all over the place. Today, thousands of rural families live on a thin strip of land that will have a house next to the road, then a vegetable garden, then a couple of fruit trees, and then the field, with perhaps one black and white cow and a few chickens. The hay is mown by men with scythes; it is women's and children's work to rake the hay. Every area has its own distinctive style of haycocks, drying the hay over wood frames or piled branches. *Powiat* (small towns) come to life twice a week: on market day and on Sunday.

"I am happy to work hard as long as it is for myself and the children. Why should I break my back on something that will never be mine?"

—Bartoszek, a Polish farmer, talking about collective farming

65

A COAL MINER

"Normally I work seven-and-a-half-hour shifts, six days a week. I'm well paid, but I think we deserve it," says a miner who works at Katowice, where the mine produces high quality coal, much of it exported for use in steel works and power stations. He gets overtime rates on Sundays and 26 days' vacation a year. Like his fellow miners, he will probably go to resort houses owned by the mine on the Baltic coast, or beside the Mazurian lakes, or in the Tatra mountains. After he has worked three years at the mine, all his travel costs are paid. He will retire at 50 with a pension of nearly 100% of his working salary. His worry, as with all industrial workers, is that exports are plunging and more miners are being laid off each year.

TOWN LIFE

Rapid industrialization and urbanization since World War II have resulted in 60% of the population now living in towns. This shift from small villages to big towns has brought with it tremendous problems of housing and overcrowding. The lucky ones own a house with a bit of garden. That is why parks are so important to Poles.

Not all city dwellers live in grey industrial areas. New apartment blocks and clean suburbs are being built—at a price. The streets are litter-free, and there is hardly any graffiti. High-tech businesses are moving to computerized efficiency. But the Polish worker still needs to work, and a dirty job is better than no job at all. "If they close the mines, there will be no jobs. How will we live then?" is the worry of local workers. In the days of Communist bureaucracy, over half the urban population used to work in the countless state offices. It was state policy to create jobs even where there was no work. Now that the job market has become more realistic, many people are out of work.

Poles love the country and farming, even when they have to live in town, like the old woman looking out of her window *(opposite)*. A solution is to own an allotment or small plot of land, such as this one *(below)*, where one can grow some fruit and vegetables for the table.

LIFE IN WARSAW

Although the much-photographed, beautifully restored Old Town is the Warsaw most foreigners want to see, most Varsovians, which is what people who live in Warsaw are called, live on the outskirts of the city in the mammoth rectangular blocks of apartments that make up the uniform suburbs.

This is where Teresa lives with her mother and father and their new puppy on the eighth floor of a tower block. They are lucky to have a small apartment with two rooms, besides a bathroom and a tiny kitchen. Teresa is used to it. "At least we have a good view!" she says as she waters the flower pots on the balcony, which is their only garden. Until last year, they had to share the apartment with grandpa and grandma as well. On weekdays the city is packed. Every morning, Teresa fights her way through the rush hour traffic to catch the bus to school. Besides cars and buses, there are trams to beware of, clanging past like trains on lines down the middle of the road. She enjoys school, especially English language classes that started recently. If she stays after school for sports, which she enjoys, then she hits the evening rush hour.

Teresa is glad when Friday comes. She watches other families squeeze into their small Fiat cars and join the traffic jams on their way for a weekend in the country. She envies them a little for owning a country home, but at least she can enjoy Warsaw without them. She and her mother do their shopping on Saturday morning. Loaded down with bulging baskets, they pause for a cup of tea in a café in the Old Market Square. Teresa steals another look at the new dress her mother has bought her for that evening's dance. There were never clothes like that in the shops in the bad old years, her mother tells her. But it was still expensive. She gives her mother a special hug. In the afternoon, after her piano lesson, Teresa is busy washing her hair, with an eye too on the television because their local soccer team is playing.

On Sunday, Teresa wakes early and gazes out of her high window. The streets are almost empty. She and her parents take a bus to the Old Town for they like to attend mass in the Church of the Holy Cross. The church is as crowded as always. After that, they all go for a walk in the Saxon Gardens. At noon, they pause beside the Tomb of the Unknown Soldier to watch the ceremonial changing of the guard. Then it's home for Sunday lunch of pork and sauerkraut, and a good book in the afternoon, before she catches up on the last bits of homework for Monday.

Village musicians have extra reason to be happy when there is a wedding— they get good money for playing at the festivities.

MARRIAGE

Poles never need an excuse to celebrate, but weddings make celebration obligatory. This is all part of the deep respect for the family as a unit. To begin a new family unit—what could be more splendid? An invited guest might take three days off work to attend. A family who could not afford the cost of a wedding might sell a cow to pay for it. Young men play fiddles in the band at weddings and they get good money for this.

In the old days, a landowner's permission might be needed for a peasant to marry—and such nobility would be honored guests at the festivities. Traditional rituals include a long blessing by the parents before the actual church ceremony; greenery on the bride's headdress representing her virginity; gates of greenery through which the couple pass on their way home from church; and the ceremonial greeting of the bride by her mother-in-law with bread and salt for her new home. Obviously, such customs are not always observed today, especially in the towns where the groom wears a dark suit and the bride a white gown in Western style.

Poles believe that the success of a marriage depends on the lavishness of the hospitality and the natural gaiety of the wedding feast. The band must not stop playing, so bridesmaids feed the musicians, while others pour sips of alcohol into their mouths!

In the evening, the young couple are conducted to their bedroom to the sounds of a slow and solemn *polonaise*, danced by all the heads of families and married women present. The next morning comes the "capping" of the new bride, the first wearing of the traditional headgear that shows she has joined the ranks of married people. By custom, the bride tries to put off that moment: she defends herself and throws off the

cap; finally she agrees with much bitter sobbing, to show her reluctance to leave her family. This solemn ritual is no place for frivolous hops or laughter, even though the *polonaise* is a dance and a song combined. The *polonaise* and "capping," like many other traditional rituals, are seldom observed by modern couples.

THE LAST DAYS

The family unit remains important to Poles throughout life, so there are few homes for the aged: old relatives are looked after by the family. Grandparents look after the children after school until the parents return from work. When there was a death in the family, tradition required relatives to wear black for a year. Nowadays a black mourning band suffices. Much money is spent on graves and tombstones. After the funeral, the wake is another good Polish party. It is a spontaneous celebration of someone's life: there will be tribute speeches and toasts.

A young girl visits a cemetery in Wroclaw. Much money is spent on graves and tombstones. A Polish cemetery is always bright with flowers.

RELIGION

THE CATHOLIC FAITH is central to the life of the Polish people. They count their history as starting when King Mieszko I was publicly baptized and so adopted Christianity for Poland in the year A.D. 966.

Pope John Paul II is Polish. It must please him immensely that his own country probably has a higher proportion of Roman Catholics than any other country in Europe, except Vatican City itself. About 95% of Poles are staunch Roman Catholics.

Opposite: **Inside the impressive basilica of Jasna Gora, the holiest shrine in Poland.**

Below: **Nuns are a common sight in Poland.**

FIERCE CATHOLICS

Throughout history, Poland has been a fiercely defended outpost of Christian Europe. Gniezno, capital of the early Polish kingdom 1,000 years ago, is where Christianity was first established among the Slavic people.

As Christianity spread through the Roman world, differences of opinion arose between east and west. In A.D. 1054, the Orthodox Church broke its ties with Rome. The Russian church aligned itself with the Orthodox movement, but Poland stayed firmly aligned with Rome.

Persecution can strengthen faith, and in the case of Poland, four decades of Communist efforts against all religion were a complete failure. Instead, those years saw a religious revival—linked joyously with the appointment of a Polish pope. The Solidarity trade union was seen as an expression of the Christian values of cooperation and the dignity of work. There are more than 14,000 churches and chapels throughout the country, 2,500 convents with 28,000 nuns, and more than 500 monasteries. There are over 26,000 priests in Poland.

CHURCH AND LIFE

Each Sunday throughout Poland, the churches are overflowing. A church may have three or four church services or masses, each fully attended. Country roads can be blocked for miles with processions on festival days. Many carry multicolored banners with appeals to the Virgin Mary embroidered in gold and silvery thread: "Holy Mary, Mother of God, protect us; do not abandon us, we are your children."

Thousands of shrines line country lanes and road crossings, bright with ribbons and garlands. In winter, people trudge through the mud and snow, lovingly decorating shrines with twining boughs and paper flowers. If the shrine carries a cross, it is to commemorate a death; if it has the Madonna figure, it celebrates healing or a life saved. Every Polish home has an icon of the Virgin on the wall or a portrait of John Paul II—or both. Every village has the church as its heart.

The Roman Catholic obligation to attend mass is accepted as a joyous gathering in Poland. Each Sunday is a holy day of obligation—and so are major Christian festivals. Poles see nothing strange in this outward show of religious enthusiasm or duty. You are likely to find people at prayer in almost every church. Poland's 1,000th anniversary as a Christian country was in 1966.

Religion is not a comfort merely to older Poles. Many young people in Poland go to services, and take part in church affairs. But it is fair to say that Polish Roman Catholicism is entrenched and conservative. Such modern topics as abortion, AIDS, and homosexuality are regarded with almost superstitious horror.

This shrine is one of thousands that line the roads. They are lovingly cared for, and often adorned with ribbons and garlands.

TWO MODERN MARTYRS

STEFAN WYSZYNSKI In 1952, Cardinal Wyszynski, the primate of the Catholic Church in Poland, was exiled to a monastery as part of the Communist attack on the Church. Then, in October 1956, came the turnaround. The Polish party leader, Gomulka, needed Wyszynski's support, so he freed him. Wyszynski promptly demanded that the teaching of religion be reinstated in schools, that religious publications be restarted, and that imprisoned priests be released. All his demands were granted.

It was a strange partnership. The old-time Communist and the saintly cardinal were the only two leaders the Poles would trust. Wyszynski was not supporting the Communist regime: he was supporting national survival. Unity was of supreme importance. Without Wyszynski, much of the Polish spirit would never have survived. His vital work continued through further years of protest, right up to the formation of Solidarity.

Cardinal Wyszynski (left) with Pope John Paul II when the latter was Cardinal Karol Wojtyla, archbishop of Cracow. "In my Poland there is not enough room in the churches for the faithful," said Cardinal Wyszynski when he visited Rome in 1957.

JERZY POPIELUSZKO From humble beginnings, a farmer's son became a fiery pro-Solidarity preacher. Such outspoken comment in the days of martial law was an embarrassment to the state. On October 19, 1984, Father Jerzy Popieluszko was abducted and murdered by security forces. The nation was shocked. In the abduction process, the priest's driver escaped, so details of what happened became known. To everyone's surprise, the government brought the murderers to trial and the two ringleaders were jailed for 25 years. Popieluszko's funeral became a Solidarity demonstration. The grave and church of Popieluszko at St. Stanislaw Kostka in Zoliborz, in northern Warsaw, remain Solidarity shrines.

Jesus said that He had come as the "Light of the World." Polish churches have rows of lighted candles before the image of the Blessed Virgin Mary or the patron saint of that particular church. Worshipers often buy a candle in church as a form of alms-giving and leave it lit as a sign of their special prayer.

POLAND'S FIRST POPE

When Karol Wojtyla appeared on the steps of St. Peter's Basilica in Rome as Pope John Paul II, his first words were *Non abbiate paura!* (Be not afraid!) It was 1978. Poland was in the grip of food shortages and price increases, strikes and arrests. Pope John Paul II believed his election as pope was some form of divine compensation for the sufferings of Poland.

Karol Wojtyla was baptized on June 20, 1920, in Wadowice, about 20 miles southwest of Cracow. He lost his mother at a very early age. After his elder brother's death from scarlet fever at the hospital where the brother was working as a doctor, Wojtyla grew up a motherless only child. His father became an admirable stabilizing influence. Wojtyla recalls how seeing his father on his knees in prayer had a decisive influence on his early years. Sadly, his father died during the war, under the Nazi occupation. Wojtyla was not yet 21 and had already lost all the people he loved.

He was at the Jagiellonian University in Cracow when the teachers were deported to concentration camps. He chose to train as a priest, which could only be done in the strictest secrecy. In order to stay in that area, where college teaching was still done in secret, Wojtyla worked in a stone quarry that supplied the sulfur factory in the district of Cracow. As his mother had hoped, Wojtyla became a priest and his career prospered.

On October 16, 1978, it was announced that Cardinal Wojtyla, Archbishop of Cracow, had been elected Holy Father of the Roman Catholic Church, becoming Pope John Paul II. He was the Pope of a Christian renewal—the first Slav pope.

John Paul II rises at 5:45 a.m.—not very easily, he admits. He says mass at 7 a.m., after a long meditation. There may be a short audience before breakfast, at which there is always one or more guests. From 9 to 11 a.m.

he is in his office, and no visitors are permitted. In the old days in Cracow, he would often lock himself in his chapel so he could write for two hours undisturbed. From 11 a.m. to 1:30 p.m., he receives visitors, then lunches with more guests. He may take half an hour's rest before going to the terrace to say his prayers. Then until 6:30 p.m. he works in his office with his assistants. Ministers and senior civil servants may try to interrupt him. Dinner (called "supper" in the Vatican) is at nearly 8 p.m. At 9 p.m. the Pope retires to his chapel again to pray. Often he goes to bed only after 11 p.m.

He made papal visits to Poland in 1979, 1983, and 1987, to emphasize that the Church truly ruled in Poland, not Communism. Millions of people traveled to see and hear him preach. There was a great surge of joy throughout the country. The happiness of a whole people could be read on their faces. The Pope's native land remains dear to his heart. When he was in the hospital, recovering from an attempt on his life, he had a big picture of Czestochowa placed on the wall facing his bed.

THE BLACK MADONNA

The holiest shrine in Poland is Jasna Gora, the Shining Mountain, the Pauline monastery at Czestochowa. The chapel of Jasna Gora houses the miraculous image of the Black Madonna, Poland's most treasured icon (the picture on the right shows a replica). According to legend, this image was painted by St. Luke on a table top of dark cypress wood made by St. Joseph himself. Its "black" quality is merely the aging of the pigments used. Rescued from the ruins of Jerusalem in A.D. 70, the icon was taken to Byzantium, presented to King Constantine, and in the 14th century presented to the Polish King Casimir who put it in Czestochowa for safe keeping. Brigands once tried to steal the picture, but when they reached the German border, their horses, "moved by a miraculous force," refused to go any farther. So the picture was returned to the monastery.

Poles believe the real miracle took place about 350 years ago when a Swedish invasion swept over Poland but failed to capture the monastery. The monks, with a handful of Polish troops, held out until the Swedish commander called off the siege as his soldiers refused to go on fighting. They swore that "their own bullets came back at them, bouncing off the monastery walls." They said they saw a woman in a blue cloak floating above the shrine and covering the fortress with her mantle. They were convinced that heavenly forces were on the side of the monks.

Perhaps even more miraculously, the shrine of the Black Madonna emerged safely from both Nazi and Communist occupations.

Every August, 100,000 pilgrims crowd into Czestochowa and visit the high-domed Gothic chapel to kneel before the black and silver altar of the Virgin. The walls are hung with countless offerings in gratitude for healing miracles—silver plaques with a name and date, shaped like a heart, an eye, a limb, or even discarded crutches.

SOME PLACES OF WORSHIP

Poland today has more churches and priests than before the war, many monasteries, and about 30,000 nuns, many working in the community. In such a religious-minded nation, it is not surprising that there are some very impressive places of worship.

Most unusual must be the underground Chapel of the Blessed Kings hewn in crystal rock at the ancient salt mine of Wieliczka. Everything in the large ornate chapel is carved from salt: stairs, bannisters, altar, and chandeliers. The acoustics are so perfect that the chapel is also used now for concerts.

In Cracow is the Church of St. Andrew, topped with twin Baroque spires. The silver pulpit inside is a masterpiece in the shape of a ship manned by angelic mariners, as is often the case in Polish churches. Nuns attend services hidden behind a grille in the gallery.

On the Silver Mountain (so called because of the silver bark of the birch trees) west of Cracow stands the church and hermitage of the Camaldolese monks at Bielany. Here lives a strict monastic order from Italy whose motto is *Memento mori* (Remember you must die). Monks live in seclusion, dressed in cream-colored robes, each with his own tiny cottage and vegetable garden that is his only source of food. They meet for common meals only five times a year. Except for times of prayer, they maintain a vow of silence. The white limestone church and the crypt (where bodies are sealed inside stone niches) may be visited by men, but women are only admitted on major religious festivals.

"Communism comes and goes, but the Catholic Church is here to remain."

—*Cardinal Stefan Wyszynski*

The Church of St. Andrew in Cracow.

THE CHURCH VERSUS COMMUNISM

How can Catholics be Communists? They can't. The disciples of Lenin do not admit the existence of God. But a Communist would find it very difficult to ignore a religious holiday in Poland. They would be fully aware of the rejoicing and worship. Catholicism has been so deeply woven into Poland's national life that it is impossible for anyone living in Poland to escape it. Perhaps the Polish Church has played its part in bringing awareness of religion to those without it. Certainly, those Poles forced to pay lip service to the state were Catholics first and nominal Communists a distant second.

Although the Communists claimed that they practiced "religious toleration," the Church maintained that there was an official conspiracy to enforce atheism. The Church vigorously defended the political rights of all Poles as well. Cardinal Wyszynski, head of the Catholic Church, and Karol Wojtyla, archbishop of Cracow and later Pope John Paul II, preached that the government had to respect the people's right to participate in the political and social life of Poland. The Church became a symbol of resistance against the system. The more the Polish people suffered, the more they found in religion an inexhaustible source of strength. That is why Communism lost its battle with the Church.

A priest blesses religious articles brought by worshipers.

RELIGIOUS TOLERANCE

Although open-minded in most matters, Poles cling to a fairly narrow view when it comes to religion. A Protestant can be regarded as a foreigner. Yet Poland used to be famous for its religious tolerance. Those with unorthodox beliefs, whether Christian or not, found hospitality here.

It was to Poland that the oppressed Jews of Western Europe came for a haven, followed by the persecuted Bohemian Brotherhood (a Christian group formed in Bohemia in 1467). For several centuries, Poland had Europe's greatest concentration of Jews, secure in their own religious, cultural, and intellectual life. Today, you will still find places of worship for Protestants, Catholics, Jews, Moslems, and Buddhists. You will see churches of the Eastern Orthodox creed with their double-barred, slanting crucifix.

Yet suspicion of those with a different faith is deep-rooted in Poland's history. In 1668, the Sejm declared that anybody who converted from Catholicism to another branch of Christianity would be exiled. Non-Catholics could not become Polish nobles—and thus members of the Sejm. Of course, not everybody obeyed such rules.

Poles today are free to worship as they please. Poland has perhaps a million non-Catholic believers, including an established Protestant Lutheran church. There are a small number of Methodists and Baptists, and even a few thousand Muslim Tartars, but the Roman Catholic Church remains monolithic.

Political parties abound. Yet the suspicion of those who do not conform has been sadly strengthened by those very Communist years Poland is trying so hard to forget.

The Communist asked, "Why is it, Father, that when you ring the bells for service all the villagers come running, but when I call a party meeting hardly anyone shows up?" The priest replied, "That's easy to answer. You and I both promise the people paradise, but you have already given them a taste of yours."

—an apocryphal story

LANGUAGE

POLISH IS A WESTERN SLAVIC LANGUAGE, together with Czechoslovakian, Slovakian, and Serbian. Russian, although written in the very different Cyrillic alphabet, also belongs to the same Slavic language group. This double group of languages, often known as Balto-Slavic, is spoken by about 300 million people, more than half of whom speak Russian. As the Polish language differs slightly in different areas, the standard form of Polish is based on the dialect of Poznan in west Poland. Not everyone in Poland speaks Polish as a home language. The Ukrainians and Belorussians are bilingual. They speak Polish well, yet their respective home languages mark them as a separate language group.

LANGUAGE UNITES A NATION

Polish uses the same alphabet as West European languages with the exception of one letter and some accents, which are explained in the next section. This was determined by Poland's close association with the Roman Catholic Church and the use of the Latin language for worship—and therefore for writing. The earliest recorded use of Polish appears in 12th century church documents. There are numerous hymns, sermons, psalters, and law court records dating from the early Middle Ages (14th and 15th centuries). Despite the fall of the Polish state in the late 18th century, Polish culture continued to develop. Language united the nation, yet localized country dialects reflecting former tribal patterns remain significant. There are, for example, clearly recognized dialects known as Great Polish, Silesian, Little Polish, and Mazovian. Poles from Warsaw will find it hard to understand the local chatter in a Tatra mountain village.

Opposite: **Poles sit and chat at an open-air café.**

Below: **Women spend time together. Not everyone in Poland speaks Polish at home, but it is a language that all speak well.**

SLAVS

No one quite knows how or where the Slav people originated. It is thought that, way back in prehistoric times, they settled in what is now western Russia and eastern Poland. Today, the majority of Poles and Czechoslovaks are Slavs. Those who lived on the *po-more* or "sea coast" were called Pomeranians; those who lived in the *pole* or "open country" were known as Polyanians. That could be where the name Poland comes from.

The original word Slav is said to have come either from *slava* meaning "glory" or from *slovo* meaning "speech." However, it was common in early medieval times for powerful mid-European nations to capture Slav children as servants. The word Slav (whether *sklave* in German, or *slaaf* in Dutch, or *esclave* in French) then took on a new meaning: "slave."

LANGUAGES IN EDUCATION

There have been times in Polish history when it was forbidden for the Polish language to be used in schools and offices. Adam Mickiewicz, one of Poland's most admired poets, grew up in the 1820s, when the imperial Russian government was determined to eliminate the Polish language and all its cultural heritage. To succeed, a Pole was expected to learn Russian and convert to Greek Orthodoxy.

Similarly, under the recent Communist domination, the Russian language had to be taught in all schools from grade 5 up to 12, and a course in Russian was compulsory in any degree course. For the Poles, their language has become more than just a means of communication; it is a symbol of the continued existence of the Polish nation. When the state tried to fill the Polish language with "official" new words and expressions, the Poles developed their own underground version of their language in which they could voice their hatred of Russian domination.

The third language offered for instruction in Communist-controlled Polish schools was French. But the Poles of today see no need for that either. They want to learn English, since it is a global language, and German, since they need economic ties with their western neighbor. In fact, English is becoming seen as a sign of sophistication! You learn English as a status symbol and to help your career prospects. The teaching of English has become one of the most thriving businesses in Poland.

EXPRESSIONS IN COMMON USE

If you hear a Pole saying "Jane dobray," it is not your name that is pronounced incorrectly. The Pole is saying *Dzien dobry* ("gen DO-bri"), which means "Good morning." Before a drive, a Pole may wish you *Szerokiej drogi* ("sh-ROK-yay DRO-gi"), which suggests the pleasant notion, "Have a wide road!"

A familiar form of greeting used among friends and relations is *ty* (like the French *tu* or German *du*). However, this is not used when greeting older people or those in important positions: for *them* the correct form of address is *Pan* (Sir) for a man or *Pani* (Madam) for a woman. It is impolite to use a surname when addressing someone you know. There is automatic respect for those with professional qualifications: a doctor will be greeted as *Panie doktorze* (Sir doctor).

Here are some common Polish expressions:

Tak (tack) = Yes

Nie (NEE-ah) = No

Prosze (PRO-shay) = Please

Dziekuje (gen-COO-yea) = Thank you

Przepraszam (puh-shay-PRUSH-am) = Sorry, or excuse me

Do widzenia (do vitz-ZAN-ia) = Goodbye

Some words you will recognize easily, like "auto," "hotel," and "stop." Many of the familiar greetings come from the strong religious element in Polish life. Villagers greet each other with "May Jesus Christ be praised," to which the response will be "Forever and ever." It is hardly surprising that *Szczesc Boze* (shCHEch BOH-zher, meaning "God bless you!") is the typical Polish "goodbye."

A Polish newspaper. The Polish language has not been through the modernizing and simplifying process of many other European languages.

PRONUNCIATION

A few words in Polish go a long way in making friends, so it is worth the trouble of sorting through what may look like a jumble of consonants without vowels. There are, in fact, 45 sounds transcribed by 32 letters.

As in English, there are three genders—masculine, feminine, and neuter—that create different cases and structures for some verbs, as well as nouns and adjectives. Nouns may change with a preceding preposition as in Latin: so *miasto* is the Polish for "town," but "to the town" is *do miasta*.

The complexity of grammar goes back to the time when Poland was wiped off the map. Teachers were determined to save every single detail of their old language. As a result, Polish has not really been through the modernizing and simplifying process of so many other European languages. Polish may look complicated, but the sounds made by each letter are at least consistent. The stress (beat) always falls on the next to last syllable.

Vowels are of even length and are pronounced as follows:

a   as in "sum"
e   as in "ten"

i   as in "ease"

o   as in "lot"

u   as in "book"

y   as in "sit"

There are three specifically Polish vowels:

ą   : nasalized, as with French *on*

ę   : nasalized, as with French *un*

ó   : the same as Polish *u*

There is also the diphthong *ie* which is pronounced "y-e", so that *nie wiem* (I don't know) sounds like "NY-e VY-em"

Consonants sound mostly the way they do in English, except for the following:

c   is pronounced "ts" or "tz"

j   is soft, as in "yes"

w   sounds like "v"

A Polish mailbox. The words on it are just a jumble of consonants for someone who does not speak Polish.

As in German (which is a neighboring language), some consonants are softened when they come at the end of a word. So *b, d, g, w, z* become *p, t, k, f, s* respectively. Beware of *ch*, which has the guttural sound of the Scots word *loch,* and the accented *ń* goes wobbly as in "canyon" or the Spanish *mañana.* The fearsome-looking combination of consonants *szcz* is easy to cope with if you remember the words "push chair" and use the "sh-ch" bit in the middle.

Polish also has a specially marked letter with a stroke across it: ł. This sounds like "w" and has the effect of making Władysław sound like VOOADYSOOAV, and Łódz sounds like WOOTJ because ó with that accent on sounds like "oo." There's also *ć*, which makes the "ch" sound as in "church." To pronounce the name of the founding leader of Solidarity, Lech Wałesa, say LE(ch) vaWENsa.

Like their fellow Europeans, Poles like to gesticulate with their hands as they talk.

HANDS UP!

Poles shake hands at every meeting, even with lifelong friends. Warm friendship gets an embrace as well. The older or more senior person will give the first greeting, and expects a similarly courteous reply. A woman may hold out her hand for the man to kiss in greeting. "I kiss your hand," he says, in old-style courtesy. In the street, a man always walks on the left of the woman.

Europeans tend to use their hands freely as they talk, while English-speakers often put their hands in their pockets! Poles gesticulate in much the same way as the French and Italians. Just occasionally, such sign language can be misunderstood. When Polish soldiers and airmen reached England during World War II, they happily gave the V-sign for victory. Unfortunately, the Polish sign is the opposite of the British one (the back of the hand is shown), and some people thought they were being rude!

Poles hold their fists with the thumbs concealed as a good luck gesture, indicating "I'm holding thumbs for you." To show that they think someone is crazy, Poles don't swirl a finger at their temple in American style, they tap the middle of the forehead with the index finger. At many crossroads in rural Poland, there are wooden crosses displayed. A woman coming to the crossroads will make the sign of the cross as a sign of faith.

There is a mildly rude gesture of defiance made by brandishing a fist and grabbing the inside of the elbow with the other hand as you do so. This is known as the "Kozakiewicz gesture"—in affectionate memory of the Polish pole-vaulter who was greeted with boos by the Russians at the 1980 Olympics in Moscow. Having made the jump that earned him the gold medal, he turned to the Russian crowd in full view of the TV cameras and made this sign.

Don't be surprised if a Polish woman makes the sign of the cross when she comes to a cross-roads. It is a sign of faith.

THE ARTS

ALTHOUGH THINGS ARTISTIC in Poland come originally from Slavic tradition (Eastern European and Russian), the historical involvement with Western Europe has resulted in a healthy mixture of styles. Dominated geographically and politically by Russia and Germany, Poland has looked farther west for its artistic model. France is the "cultural home" of Poles. It was in Paris that Chopin wrote most of his music and Marie Curie isolated radium.

PART OF PRIDE AND PROTEST

When Poland disappeared off the map of Europe at the close of the 18th century, literature and art took over the role of preserving the nation and its identity. Similarly, during the repressive four and a half decades of Communist control, protest against the state was voiced chiefly through theater and painting. The rich folklore skills of costume, dance, and decorative arts were kept alive in local regions, but the dull demands of industrialization led to a decline in these old traditions. Today, tourists are encouraging fresh creativity on commercial terms, although it seems that the last generation of home-bred artists and artisans is dying out.

Among the specialities from particular regions are the painting on glass of the Zakopane mountain folk, red sequined Cracow folk costumes, Silesian brass bands, black pottery of Kielce, lacework from Koniakow, rainbow-hued cloth from Lowicz, and paper cutouts from Kurpie. The tiny village of Zalipie is famous for the flower paintings that decorate its wooden houses, wells, wagons, and wash bowls!

Opposite: **Concerts are regularly held at the base of the Chopin monument in Warsaw.**

Below: **A child's painted chair. Flower motifs are a trademark of Polish handicraft.**

A LAND OF MUSIC

Music is vibrantly alive in Poland. Such names as Frederic Chopin, Ignacy Jan Paderewski, and Artur Rubinstein are known worldwide. Poland boasts 10 symphony orchestras. International competitions—such as the Frederic Chopin piano competition and the Henryk Wieniawski violin competition—give added stimulus. There are 17 conservatories, over 100 music schools, and almost 1,000 music centers, as well as many societies and magazines devoted to music. Warsaw stages nightly performances of opera and ballet, chamber concerts, and recitals, and plays host to the Jazz Jamboree, the oldest and most celebrated jazz festival in Eastern Europe. The National Philharmonic Orchestra performs regularly.

Of course, it all started with village musicians. Music based on the fiddle, the pan pipes, or the single-reed bagpipe (and in the Kurpie forest region, an accordion with a foot pump) created the dance rhythms of the *mazurka* and *polka*. In many Polish villages they are still played in the traditional style, often for weddings and festivals. There is a folk festival each year at Kazimierz on the banks of the Vistula River that is very popular, and plenty of young people take part.

FAMOUS MUSICIANS

ARTUR RUBINSTEIN was a delightful, slightly old-fashioned showman who was, for many years, the world's best-loved pianist. A Polish Jew, Rubinstein chose to play the music that brought him success and avoided anything that might not go down well with the public. He often played the music of Brahms, Schumann, and Chopin and his recordings, recorded directly with no chance to

A jazz club in Cracow. Jazz is popular in Poland.

insert corrections as modern musicians do, remain dazzling. He enjoyed his fame and apparently liked Havana cigars, *foie gras*, lobster, caviar, old claret, and above all piano-playing and women.

WITOLD LUTOSLAWSKI was a Polish composer born in 1913. Considered now more "of the older generation" than such up-and-coming composers as Penderecki, Gorecki, and Krauze, Lutoslawski is still highly popular with concert-goers. His *Variations on a Theme of Paganini* was written in 1941, during the Nazi occupation of Warsaw. As a café pianist, he used to play piano duets with a friend after working hours, thus creating this piece. But he is best known for his stunning *Cello Concerto*, which is crammed with orchestral exuberance.

FREDERIC CHOPIN (1810–1849) made his debut as a pianist at the age of 8. The son of a French father and a Polish mother, he made his home in Paris and became well known in fashionable salons as both composer and pianist. Although his self-imposed exile was forced on him by the Russian invasion of Warsaw, Chopin's homesickness for Poland remained his inspiration. It is told how he left home at dusk, the hour of *zal*—which is also the Polish word for homesickness. He revolutionized the technique of piano playing, concentrating on bravura solo pieces. His compositions for piano were characterized by an unusual lyrical and poetic quality. Chopin died on October 17, 1849, and was buried in Paris.

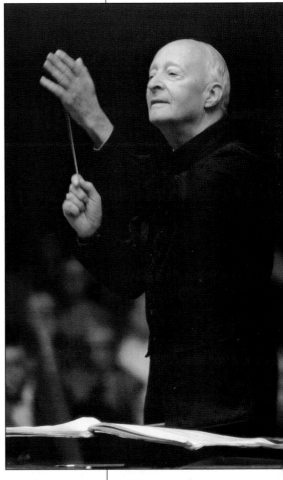

Lutoslawski (above) once said: "For me, music is something of immeasurable importance; it is a need as basic as water and air."

LITERATURE

This bookstall is over-flowing with books. Poles are avid readers.

The earliest traces of Polish folklore and legend are preserved from medieval times. There exists, for example, the hymn chanted by King Jagiello's army before their victory over the Teutonic Knights at the Battle of Grunwald in 1410. Texts of Polish folk plays survive from the Renaissance.

The first public reference library on the European mainland was the collection of Bishop Zaluski, which he donated to the Polish nation in 1747. The Sejm soon ordered printers to donate to the library the first copy of any book, and by the time the library was looted by the Russians in 1795, it contained over 500,000 volumes.

Writers are important people in Poland. Adam Mickiewicz, a 19th century poet, has the status of a national hero. He wrote of Poland at a time of her darkness and kept the flame of her spirit alive. Streets and squares are named after him. His *Pan Tadeusz* and other works exerted a strong influence on future generations.

Polish-born prose writers have won Nobel Prizes for literature: Henryk Sienkiewicz for *Quo Vadis,* a story set in the times of the Roman emperor Nero, Wladyslaw Reymont for *Chlopi,* an epic novel of Poland, strong with local color and historical detail, and Czeslaw Milosz for his poetry. Few people realize that Joseph Conrad, the popular author of English seafaring novels such as *Lord Jim,* was actually Josef Korzeniowski, born of Polish parents in the Ukraine.

Although curbs on writers were strong, Communist culture encouraged books. In 1980, for instance, 11,315 different titles were published and 141.3 million books were printed, including 50 million fiction titles and 36.8 million school books. Today, the public libraries remain popular.

Poles like books. Bookstalls spill out onto the sidewalks and reading is a popular activity. It is a pity that the present economic climate forces booksellers to pay cash for any books they put into stock. This, in turn, means most bookshops stock only what is guaranteed to sell—and that results in a high proportion of romance series and thrillers by writers like Wilbur Smith and Jeffrey Archer, all translated into Polish.

CZESLAW MILOSZ

The Polish writer Czeslaw Milosz delighted his country by winning the Nobel Prize in 1980 and subsequently returning home after 30 years in exile. Born in 1911, half Polish, half Lithuanian, Milosz was educated in France but spent the war years in Poland, active in Warsaw's underground resistance movement. Hopeful of change, he joined the Polish diplomatic service. Then disillusioned with the Communist regime, he went to teach Polish literature at the University of California.

A poet with a profound sense of vocation, he questions:
"I, who am I, a believer, dancing before the All-Holy?"
Then he answers his own question:
"A believer:
Though of weak faith, I believe in forces and powers
Who crowd every inch of the air ..."

"Poland drives out all its talented people. Frederic Chopin never saw this country again after the age of 20. He wrote all his great works abroad. Adam Mickiewicz wrote his Pan Tadeusz *in exile. Marie (Curie) Sklodowska won her two Nobel Prizes in Paris not Poland."*

—*James A. Michener in* Poland

93

THE POLISH PANORAMA

Perhaps the most spectacular aspects of Polish art are very small or very big. Tiny figures carved from prehistoric amber or delightful colored paper cutouts are part of a long folk-art tradition.

Small and intricate Polish handicrafts on display in Warsaw's Old Town Square.

In contrast are the massive canvases depicting decisive moments of Polish history such as the *Battle of Grunwald* by Jan Matejko or the more intimate paintings of Jozef Simmler.

Perhaps the greatest Polish painter is Jacek Malczewski (1854–1929) whose disturbing paintings concern "the long period of darkness" that Poland endured in the 19th century. His *Sunday in a Mine* shows a group of Polish dissidents who have been sent to Siberia.

Under the Communist regime, there was an insistence upon "socialist realism"—photographic representations of heroic generals and bright-faced workers. Polish artists hated this and reacted by turning to abstract techniques. Victor Gorka and others expressed their individuality in obscure suggestive vagueness. Freed now from both state censorship and the need for wild freedom, Polish art is exploring new themes. Marian Kruczek is typical of such thinking. He makes insect-like sculptures from scrap steel and plaster.

JAN PIENKOWSKI

This Polish-born artist remembers only too well how his family left his native Warsaw with Nazi bombs and shells falling all around.

A devout Catholic, Pienkowski has illustrated two superb picture books—one on *Christmas*, the other on *Easter*—using delicate black silhouette figures against color-washed skies. Anxious to make the story accessible to modern children, he shows Mary hanging up the washing as the Archangel Gabriel appears. "Maybe," he says, "this picture was based on an old Polish country saying that the sun shines when the Virgin hangs up her washing." He sent a copy of *Christmas* to the Pope, with a letter in Polish: he received a reply from the Vatican, also in Polish, conveying the papal blessing on his work.

CINEMA

Polish movies retained world admiration despite the state control and censorship that led to many top-class directors moving overseas. Poland's first movie-production company was Sphinx. It was launched in 1909 and managed to remain active in the inter-war period. After World War II, Polish movies had a series of international successes from such directors as Andrzej Wajda and Andrzej Munk.

Polish movie director Roman Polanski suffered a horrific childhood in Nazi-occupied Poland. Later, his wife, actress Sharon Tate, was murdered. It is hardly surprising that his movies show a fascination with horror: *Repulsion* (1965), *Rosemary's Baby* (1968), and a gory version of *Macbeth*.

Movie director Jerzy Skolimowski lived in Warsaw during the German occupation. He needed to be self-reliant very early: his father died in a concentration camp and his mother was a teacher busy with underground activities, so Skolimowski grew up in an orphanage. By the time he passed the entrance exams to the State Higher Theatrical and Film School in 1959, he had already worked as a co-author with the famed Polanski. Doomed in Poland to make movies with low budgets, he moved abroad and describes himself now as "a man with a suitcase." Such movies as *Walk-Over, Barrier*, and *Start* have won several movie festival prizes. Poland has 892 cinemas but attendance is being adversely affected by the growing popularity of television. Whereas the average Pole in 1985 used to attend the cinema 2.8 times a year, that figure by 1991 was down to 0.5.

One of the earliest movie cameras was made by a Pole, Piotr Lebiedzinski, in 1893.

THEATER

Live theater has always been welcomed in Poland. English traveling players used to visit there. German translations of Shakespeare were being performed in Gdansk even during Shakespeare's lifetime.

After the downfall of the Polish state, the theater played an enormous part in the survival of the Polish language and spirit. As in other countries, political protest was often made through the medium of drama.

During the 1960s, the Polish Laboratory Theater (the "Theater of 13 Rows") in Wroclaw gained an international reputation for its experimental work. Under director Jerzy Grotowski, it toured Western Europe and the United States, and was acclaimed an important new direction in theater.

In January 1968 the Communist authorities closed down a production of *Forefather's Eve*, a play by the poet Adam Mickiewicz. Poles revered his work and protested violently when the play was banned as anti-Russian.

Social comment is found on both sides of the footlights, for audiences are encouraged to respond vigorously. Irony and satire are strong elements in Polish theater today. Working now in the United States, Polish playwright Janusz Glowacki uses shrewd observations on life in Communist Eastern Europe to entertain American theater-goers. In *Antigone in New*

MUSHROOM SATIRE

In the 1960s, a popular act from the Student Satirical Theater in Warsaw featured a middle-aged man with a basket of mushrooms meeting a modern youth. It is clear that the man has been in the forest since September 1939. He becomes increasingly disturbed to hear what has been happening in Poland since then. "Don't worry. It's all right," the young man assures him. But the mushroom gatherer grabs his basket and heads back into the forest and into the past. "Wait a minute," says the young man. "I'm coming with you." He winks at the audience. "I have to convince him," he adds.

York, a defiant Polish thief and a depressed Russian drunk are homeless New Yorkers determined to express their defiance of "the authorities."

There are three drama schools in Poland and admission is hard to obtain. Poles flock to live entertainment at the country's 91 theaters (including 24 puppet theaters), 19 opera and musical theaters, and 21 concert halls. Warsaw's Grand Theater also houses an impressive Theater Museum.

THE MEDIA

Poles tend to compare everything today with what it was like under Communist control. In 1980, 82 newspapers and 2,550 periodicals were being published. But all of them and the radio and television networks were controlled tightly by the state. Today, the interest in daily affairs is keen. Many towns have their own daily papers; many state-owned organizations publish daily or weekly journals. Newspapers reach about one-fifth of the population. An English-language paper, *The Warsaw Voice,* has recently been launched to a warm reception.

There are eight million television sets, about one for every four people. There are still only two local television channels, but more satellite equipment is gradually making reception of Western programs possible. Imported movies are sometimes shown with a single voice translation in Polish (for all the characters!) while the original soundtrack is audible in the background. This makes listening a chore. Video rental shops do good business, however.

A Polish theater. Poles enjoy live entertainment at the country's 91 theaters.

FROM AUSTERE TO ORNATE

A street corner decoration. Old Polish buildings are often decorated with such lavish detail.

Within a country so often fought over, invaded, destroyed, and rebuilt, one must expect a variety of architectural styles. There are stern Romanesque churches, spired and fluted late-Gothic cathedrals, warm brick-built town halls, ornate masterpieces of the Italian Renaissance and Baroque styles. Poles of the 16th and 17th centuries admired the beauty of Islamic art, which complemented the popular Baroque architecture. Eastern textiles replaced Flemish tapestries on the walls of manor houses. Onion-shaped turrets topped circular towers in the style of minarets.

The Poles themselves live comfortably amid the confusion of gaunt "socialist realism" and the decorative relics of Polish history. They are more aware than the average tourist just how many of what seem historical buildings are actually clever reconstructions—especially in Warsaw. There, the Baroque Church of the Holy Cross was totally rebuilt from paintings and old photographs after the city was destroyed in 1945. It is topped by a gigantic statue of Christ holding a cross that was brought triumphantly back from Germany where it had been destined for scrap.

Many old houses such as those in the Old Town Square in Warsaw or most of Cracow have painted facades, often imitating carved classical styles. The same *trompe l'oeil* (eye-tricking) painting was used inside many of the sumptuous palaces, including those at present being restored in Wilanow Palace, Warsaw.

WITNESSES OF HISTORY

The royal castles and palaces, like Wilanow Palace (right), are undoubtedly the jewels in the Polish architectural crown. Of these, Wawel Castle in Cracow is the most impressive. Built on a rocky embankment overlooking the Vistula River, its red-brick foundations, cream walls, and dark slate roofs mix Romanesque, Gothic, and Renaissance styles, and

its ornate reception rooms recall ages of elegance now sadly lost. Wawel is the first stop along the popular Eagle Nest Trail, a chain of medieval castles built by King Casimir the Great, which ends at the Royal Castle of Warsaw.

Perhaps even more breathtaking is the gilt and marble Baroque decoration in the bigger churches.

Although the city cathedrals and castles are undoubtedly impressive, it is the village houses that show the genuine Poland most clearly—red brick and tile, steep sloping roofs against the winter snow, and always the spire of the village church.

In Pomerania, the houses are wide but low, as if ducking to avoid the wind. In Mazuria, they are smaller, sometimes thatched. In the mountains, houses are built of wood and have a pointed roof. The ugly new cottages to be seen almost everywhere are square with flat roofs, made out of mass-produced building blocks.

One recent development is the Open-Air Museum, which gathers traditional rural architecture to preserve the actual buildings. Wooden churches, mills, houses, and barns are furnished with appropriate equipment or tools and decorated as they should be. Known as *skansens*, there are so far 29 museums of this kind.

LEISURE

EVEN IN POLAND, there are complaints that sports dominate television! Certainly, any Polish successes are given full coverage. So when Wojtek Fibak did well in international tennis, his matches were televised. As a result of the general enthusiasm, tennis courts were built in country districts and the sport is now far more popular.

SPORT FOR ALL

For many years, there was a great emphasis on sports at school, and some lucky children were sent to special schools as well for extra training. But school sports are declining as there is no longer money for equipment. There are some private sports clubs, but these are expensive and only wealthier parents can afford to pay. Swimming remains popular, as does "artistic gymnastics" and synchronized swimming. Hockey, ice-hockey, volleyball, and soccer are all popular.

Some boys attend soccer practice for perhaps an hour after school, three times a week. Others play basketball or volleyball in the park. "Streetball" is enjoyed—this is similar to basketball, but there are few players to each side (three, for example), and only one basket is used.

On Saturday mornings, part of a street may be closed off and goalposts set up for soccer. Prizes may be donated by some sportswear manufacturer. The games are played through to a much-cheered final, whether it rains or not! For adults, soccer remains the top spectator sport—like volleyball, it is played at every school.

Motorcycle racing is increasing in popularity. Big audiences turn up at local club meetings; several Polish riders have already taken part in international events.

Lots of people run for sport, from local fun runs to more serious marathon races. There is a sports stadium in most towns.

Opposite: **Hiking in the Tatra mountains is an extremely popular pastime for Poles and tourists alike. The mountain trails are spectacular.**

Hunters get ready for the hunting season that opens in early November with the fox chase, or Hubertus Run, named after St. Hubertus, the patron of all hunters.

Poles have loved their horses for centuries. In a country whose history is full of wild cavalry charges, it is hardly surprising to find many riding stables and stud farms. Poland has a long tradition of breeding Arabian horses, particularly at Janow Podlaski, close to the frontier with Russia. Horse-riding, although obviously not a cheap pastime, remains popular.

Older folk especially love rifle shooting. Almost every large town has its marksmen's society. But nowhere does it have such a colorful tradition as in Cracow where there exists "The Brotherhood of the Cock." This dates back to the days when all citizens were expected to practice their warlike skills, whether with sword, bow, or musket. In Cracow, this started a shooting competition with a wooden cock on a high pole as the target. The one to shoot off the last remaining splinter became Cock King for the year and paid no municipal taxes! Today, the Brotherhood parades through Cracow in traditional finery before going off to the military firing range for the shoot-off with target rifles.

Hunting for animals, ranging from wild boar to deer or even rabbits, and fishing for pike, bass, bream, or eel are carefully controlled; both need a permit. Poles have a traditional love of the outdoor life.

SOCCER

This is the game that all small boys play in the streets and all their fathers cheer at weekends. Poland has three soccer leagues: the first and second are national, and the third provincial. Many teams are sponsored by and named after factories. A leading club is Hutnik Warsaw, which in December 1992 signed a Russian player in exchange for a television set and a video recorder. There was a general lack of hard cash. Another Warsaw team bought a Russian player for a truckload of potatoes! The 1993 club championship was won by Legia Warsaw, beating LKS Lodz on goal average. The season lasts from March to November. Winter is too cold. The June/July vacation (the "cucumber season") is time for a rest, soccer training camps, or friendly international games.

Poland takes part regularly in international soccer tournaments and won the silver medal in the 1992 Barcelona Olympics. The following year, having drawn their home match in the World Cup against England, Polish soccer players were amused to note that England, who invented the game, then lost their own match against the United States.

POLISH OLYMPICS

The figures (right) show clearly how Poland was slow in building up to an Olympic sporting standard until the years after World War II. The leap to 21 medals in 1960 shows the emphasis placed on sport and training by the Communist regime.

After 62 nations, including the United States, boycotted the 1980 Olympics because of the Soviet invasion of Afghanistan, the Soviet Union boycotted the 1984 Olympics in Los Angeles in return. Most Communist countries, including Poland, had to follow suit.

Polish male gold medal athletes have included Bronislaw Malinowski (3,000-meter steeplechase 1980), Jacek Wszola (high jump 1976), Tadeusz Slusarski and Wladyslaw Kozakiewicz (pole vault 1976 and 1980), and Jozef Schmidt (triple jump 1960 and 1964). Among the women winners were Irena Szewinska (200 meters 1968 and 400-meter relay 1964). Poland also boasts eight gold medal boxers.

In the 1992 Olympics at Barcelona, Poland's total of 19 medals placed the country again 14th out of 64 medal-winning countries. Their prowess in boating won them three medals in the kayak events.

In the Winter Olympics held since 1924, Poland ranks 19th out of 25, with a total of only four medals.

Olympic medals won:

	G	S	B*
1924	0	1	1
1928	1	1	3
1932	2	1	4
1936	0	3	3
1948	0	0	1
1952	1	2	1
1956	1	4	4
1960	4	6	11
1964	7	6	10
1968	5	2	11
1972	7	5	9
1976	7	6	13
1980	3	14	15
1984	Soviet boycott		
1988	2	5	9
1992	3	6	10

*G = gold
S = silver
B = bronze

The skiing is excellent at the picturesque ski resort of Zakopane. Its two ski jumps are among the best in Europe.

WINTER SPORT

Skiing is Poland's most popular winter sport. Not even the dreariness of the Communist regime weakened the country's enthusiasm. When winter comes, people take an uncomfortable overnight train journey to the High Tatras, waking up to the sight of white-topped mountains and spruce forests. The Tatra range has lakes, waterfalls, hidden valleys, and a wealth of old legends. Its people are reserved and ceremonially courteous.

The picturesque ski resort of Zakopane is the winter sports capital of Poland. Its name means "a place buried in the ground," or simply "dig." Zakopane has been host to the International Ski Championship and the Olympic Winter Games. Its two magnificent ski jumps are among the best in Europe; there is a cable car up the Kasprowy (6,450 feet high) and in a good snow-filled winter as many as 50 ski lifts will be in operation. For Poles, this is not a fashion show or a demonstration of high skill: it is a time of adventure, simple accommodation, good company—and perhaps a glass of something warming by the log fire afterwards.

"When life gets unbearable, there is always Zakopane."

—Polish saying

WHAT TO DO

Public entertainment in Poland is expanding. Most towns have a cinema although the movies may be fairly old ones from the United States. Warsaw has 16 cinemas and 15 theaters. Warsaw and Lodz have fine opera houses, and there are music concerts, from classical to jazz, nearly everywhere. There isn't much dancing, except at discos, and bars are usually always expensive. Poles prefer to drink at home.

Families watch the television programs available: there are three national channels and cable and satellite television, giving Poles a.choice of 40 channels altogether. Poles often prefer just putting on some music. American pop is popular. On Mondays, theaters, museums, and everything else stay shut.

WHERE TO GO

Even Poles are starting to be tourists inside their own country. Freed from state restrictions and aided by improving transport, they are trying out more than the traditional winter sports.

There are nearly 1,000 youth hostels, more than any other country in the world, and conditions can be spartan. Many are school buildings in which desks have been replaced by beds. However, there is a full range of hotels—and many large firms retain holiday apartments that are allocated to deserving employees. The universal outdoor activity, and probably the cheapest, is hiking. Trails are well marked, and in the mountains can be spectacular.

Discos provide an outlet for young Poles, who go there to dance and enjoy popular music.

FESTIVALS

THE ANCIENT ANNUAL CYCLE of ordained church fasts and festivals remains the pattern of the year for Poles. Advent announces the coming of Christmas; Christmas celebrates the birth of Christ; Ash Wednesday begins the period of Lent recalling His fasting in the wilderness; then Palm Sunday processions welcome Holy Week, with the solemnity of Good Friday and the new birth of Easter. Scattered through the year are other important festivals, with a regular celebration once a week on Sundays.

HARVEST FESTIVAL

Although this is recognized now as the time to visit the fields and orchards to thank God for the year's harvest, the harvest traditions are far older than Christianity. Old pagan rituals were steadily stopped and forbidden during the Middle Ages, but one that survives is that of Koza, "the goat." A boy with a sheepskin over his head and shoulders and accompanied by carol singers goes visiting to bring prosperity, help the growth of the corn, and assure a successful harvest.

Opposite and above: **Poland has a rich folk dance culture and dancers like these show their skill at folk festivals.**

At the "harvest home" celebrations at the end of the season, girls carry the harvest wreath (a cone or circular shape) made of corn and topped with the figure of a cock or a girl. When the girls who carry the harvest wreath have completed their special dance, they are supposed to give the wreath to the farmer—and the next year's sowing will start with seed crumbled from the wreath made of last year's crop. A typical harvest procession of today will be led by the processional cross, flanked by choir boys in cassocks and lacy surplices, and followed by the congregation. They will visit the fields and barns to thank God for His goodness and ask for His continued bounty.

HOLY WEEK

After the self-imposed disciplines of Lent, the week that precedes Easter is a period of varied festivities. Holy Week in Poland is heralded by spring fairs, selling early-grown vegetables and livestock. These lead into Palm Sunday, which is a fine excuse for the processions Poles love. The palms may be small sprays of everlasting flowers or willow branches mixed with white catkins. In the mountain villages, men make "palms" up to 15 feet high, adorned with flowers, ribbons, and colored papers.

On Maundy Thursday there may be scenes similar to the English Guy Fawkes bonfires: some Polish communities take symbolic revenge on Judas Iscariot, hanging a stuffed figure, dragging it outside the village, and there burning it or throwing it into the river.

Good Friday is celebrated with solemn services, and then perhaps a visit to a specially created life-size portrayal of the Holy Sepulchre. In Rzeszow this has become mixed up, in local tradition, with King Jan Sobieski's victory at the Siege of Vienna, so there are Turkish soldiers on guard outside the tomb. Good Friday is a "holy day," not a holiday. Some families fast all day.

Near Cracow, there is a spectacular passion play telling the story of Christ's passion. It is as popular locally as the more famous Oberammergau cycle in Bavaria. The main parts are played by local priests, but pilgrims play the disciples, Pharisees, and soldiers. They consider this a great honor. The play visits over 20 chapels, representing the Stations of the Cross, that mark the highlights of Christ's passion, accompanied by thousands of devout spectators.

Holy Saturday is the day for mother to do the Easter baking, while her children take baskets of eggs to church to be blessed and sprinkled with holy water.

WET MONDAY

On Easter Monday, the custom of *Smigus-Dyngus* (water dousing) provides some light relief. Gangs of children armed with water-pistols, or buckets and sprays, roam the streets in search of victims. Boys chase the girls. They might use just a spray of perfume or a plastic lemon as water-pistol or a bucket of water. The first one up in the morning is supposed to have the right to spray others, who aren't supposed to fight back. They usually do! This custom originated from ritual washing, a purification intended to bring rain to fields sown with grain. Today it's thought of as a damp piece of good luck!

EASTER

This is the highlight of the Catholic year, when church services are even more crowded than usual. The Paschal Lamb takes the place of the Easter Bunny. Cakes are decorated with a lamb, made either of sugar or wood. The traditional Easter cake is *mazurek*—a thin layer of shortbread pastry with different iced flavors like chocolate, coffee, and caramel. Polish children enjoy Easter eggs as much as other children in the world. Real eggs are hardboiled and decorated. They are eaten at the Easter breakfast, after mass. The old way was to boil them with onion skins to dye them a beautiful rich brown. In western Poland, the eggs are stained a single color, but this may be red, yellow, or green; around Cracow and the south, many colors are used, sometimes with red cutout stencils; in Mazowsze, they cover the eggs with very fine linen, ornamented with the pith from bulrushes.

This is the Church of St. Peter and Paul. The feast day of these two apostles is a holy day of obligation on which Catholics have to attend mass.

HIGH DAYS AND HOLY DAYS

Roman Catholics are expected to attend mass and refrain from all unnecessary work on certain days that are known as holy days of obligation. Sunday is one of these. There are also 10 special days the Polish call High Days: Christmas, the Circumcision, the Epiphany, the Ascension, Corpus Christi, the Assumption, Saints Peter and Paul Day, All Saints Day, the Immaculate Conception, and St. Joseph's Day.

The feast of Corpus Christi ("Body of Christ") honors the "real presence of Christ" in the Eucharist, which is the bread that is distributed to Catholics during mass. It is observed with colorful processions on the Thursday after Trinity Sunday, with the Corpus Christi, the consecrated bread, held high with great reverence and rejoicing.

The 40 days preceding Easter are those of Lent—a time of fasting, when fat, butter, and eggs are forbidden. As a result, on Shrove Tuesday, the day before Lent is due to begin, all these ingredients have to be used up: pancakes seem an obvious way. In Europe this day is known as *Mardi Gras* (Fat Tuesday), when people not only feast but enjoy colorful, noisy carnivals.

The first day of Lent is Ash Wednesday, the beginning of a time of repentance. Ashes from the previous year's palm crosses are put in a bowl and sprinkled with holy water. The priest marks an ash cross with his thumb on the forehead of each worshiper as a sign of penance.

Lady Day is the traditional name for the Feast of the Annunciation of the Blessed Virgin Mary, celebrated on March 25. It recalls how the Archangel Gabriel informed Mary of the forthcoming birth of Jesus.

THE LEGEND OF THE CHRISTMAS SPIDERS

This tale came to Poland from Germany.

When Jesus was a boy—so the legend goes—he came to a poor farmhouse on Christmas Eve where the front door was closed in a most unfriendly fashion. Outside in the cold, he found a family of spiders. They were crying softly in sadness, for they had seen the Christmas tree in the house, bare and without decoration because the family could not afford such luxuries. So the boy Jesus opened the door and let the spiders in. Gladly, they hurried across the floor and swarmed all over the tree. When they had finished, its branches were festooned with their sticky grey cobwebs. The Christ Child looked at the tree. He knew that the farmer's wife kept her house spotlessly clean and had no love of cobwebs. So he blessed the tree, and the grey threads turned to strands of silver and gold. And that is why Christmas trees have shining, glistening strands of tinsel.

WE WISH YOU A MERRY CHRISTMAS

In the old tradition, a small, sweet-smelling spruce tree known as the *podlaznik* is hung from the rafters on Christmas Eve. Young women decorate it with apples, baked cookies, walnuts wrapped in shiny paper, and cutout paper patterns for stars. Others place their Christmas tree more conventionally on the floor. Young men go from house to house calling Christmas greetings, and if one of them catches a young woman under the dangling *podlaznik*, he is allowed to kiss her.

Christmas Eve (*Wigilia*) begins when the first star is sighted. Everyone changes into their best clothes, then looks for presents under the Christmas tree. The special supper will start with the sharing of bread: the father first, then his family. The meal may be fish, noodles, wild mushrooms, special cabbage, herring—but no meat. No alcohol is served either, because the whole family will go to church that night to celebrate the midnight mass.

On Christmas Day, there may be a church service again in the morning and then comes lunch—*rosol*, a clear chicken soup with macaroni, then all kinds of cold meats: ham, salami, horseradish, potatoes, and salad.

The Christmas creche is known in Poland as *szopka* (SHOP-ka). It is sometimes portrayed by moving puppets, sometimes by hand-carved wooden figures. The traditional arrangement of figures represents Herod, the Devil, Death, and the Holy Family in a scene of adoration.

FAMILY OCCASIONS

The great family occasions are baptism, first communion, and marriage. Nearly all Polish children receive first communion. This is a very important event for the whole family, relations coming from all over the country for the occasion. The child will be dressed in new clothes, often in traditional style.

Wedding anniversaries are carefully noted—for the family unit is very important in Poland—and there is an extra big party every 10 years.

Mother's Day is very important, too. Children in school may put on a special play for the occasion and invite their parents to the performance.

As in many Catholic countries, your "birthday" celebration is not on your birthday but on your Name Day. This is the feast day of the saint after whom you are named.

But the Poles don't really need an excuse for a party. One father explained, with a twinkle in his eye, "If my boy comes home from school with a good note from his teacher, then we celebrate. If he comes home without a good note, then the teacher must have forgotten to give it to him, so we celebrate anyway!"

Girls in traditional white and boys in their best suits celebrate First Holy Communion at Jasna Gore monastery.

THE ANNUAL PLEDGE

The Blessed Virgin is the patron of the Polish Crown. Poland's knights used to ride into battle singing *Bogurodzica* (Mother of God). When the Swedish troops were driven out of the country, the King of Poland pledged himself and his nation to the service of "Our Lady, Queen of the Crown of Poland." To this day, Polish Catholics annually renew their vows to her. Traditionally, this is done at the shrine of the Black Madonna at Czestochowa.

"Every day is good for celebration!"

—*Polish saying*

PUBLIC HOLIDAYS

These are the official public holidays in Poland:

January 1	New Year's Day	May or June	Corpus Christi
March	Good Friday	November 1	All Saints Day
or April	Easter Monday	November 11	National Independence Day
May 1	Workers' Day	December 25, 26	Christmas
May 3	Constitution Day		

WORKERS' DAY is increasingly celebrated all over the world. During the years of Communist control in Poland, this day was an annual reminder of the power of Moscow. But on May 1, 1984, Walesa and other Solidarity workers managed to join the state-organized May Day parade, flashing V-for-victory signs as they passed the government officials on the reviewing stand. On May Day in 1988, protests urged by Solidarity took place in 12 cities. Now, the day marks the victory of Solidarity over Communism.

CONSTITUTION DAY is the anniversary of the adoption, in 1791, of the constitution: the first in Europe and the second in the world.

FOOD

THE GUIDING PRINCIPLE OF POLISH CUISINE is to reach the heart through the stomach! As a rule, Poles eat simply but fully. Most cannot afford to eat out often, but when they do, they make the most of it. Restaurants, once open, stay open through the day. Food, to Poles, is a serious matter.

Breakfast is usually eaten around 7 a.m., and is little more than a sandwich with tea or coffee. This is often followed by a "second breakfast" around midday that is a light lunch, perhaps including fried eggs and ham or frankfurters, or else a cold plate of meats, cheese, rolls, and jam. The main hot meal is eaten in the late afternoon. There may be a snack of cold meat or cheese with bread later at night. The most important meal of the week is Sunday lunch. That goes on a long time!

BREAD AND CAKES

In Communist times, most of the bread was mass-produced, rather hard, made of rye, and often flavored with caraway seeds. Now there is an increasing number of private bakeries providing fancy loaves, croissants, and others, as well as the still popular rye bread. There's a darker brown bread flavored with honey and a white, sour rye bread that is good with cheese. Bread is only served in a restaurant if ordered, when it is paid for by the slice, but Poles eat plenty of bread at home with butter or margarine and all kinds of jam: plum, strawberry, or blackberry.

Cakes are a favorite. Even small villages have their own cake shop. *Sernik* (cheesecake) is popular everywhere, and you may also be treated to sponge cake

Opposite: **The typical cheese sold in the Zako-pane area looks almost too good to eat. It is made from goat's milk and is dry and delicious.**

Below: **Food is displayed in a shop front window: bread, cheese, fruit— everything one needs for a simple Polish meal.**

Fast-food eating is a convenient in Poland. Signs offer a choice of hamburgers, pizzas, or *flaki*, a very popular dish of tripe.

topped with plums, poppyseed cake, or the attractively colored marble cake. Feast days demand a special cake. The wedding cake is ring-shaped and studded with round cracknels and other decorations made of sweetened dough. Small cakes shaped like animals used to be thrown at the bridal couple as they returned from the wedding ceremony. Two oblong cakes, cooked together, were traditionally given to the bride and bridegroom at their first breakfast. An Easter cake is one flavored with chocolate, coconut, cream, and poppyseeds.

At a baptism, cakes four feet long are baked in the belief that the happiness and good luck of the child depends on the size of the cake. There are special rolls and cakes called *kolacz* for funerals. For All Souls Day, flat pancakes called *placki* are made.

MEAT EATERS

In spite of economic shortages, Poles have remained insatiable meat eaters. Beef and pork are their main favorites, with hams and different types of sausages for snacks through the day. The most common meat dish is a fried pork cutlet served in a thick sauce.

But because meat is still expensive, the average family serves it mostly on feast days or to visitors. Otherwise the menu is based on vegetables that

IT CAN'T BE BEETEN!

Beet is a many-purpose vegetable, a mainstay for the Polish cook. It can be served hot or cold, made into soup or pickled, and it's a healthy food, rich in potassium, calcium, and Vitamin A. Beetroot soups include the famous *barszcz* (BURshch) or borscht at it is known to Americans, a clear, spicy red beetroot soup always served with a small meat pastry like a sausage roll.

Botwinka is a soup made from the leaves of baby beetroot, served with a hard-boiled egg, and *chlodnik*, a cold pink Lithuanian soup with sour milk and crunchy strips of onion or green vegetables. The latter looks a bit like a strawberry milkshake! Only young beetroot are used, and both bulb and stem are ingredients.

Salads are made of beetroot and eye-watering horseradish. Every Polish vegetable garden will have a few rows of beetroot for the home larder.

are mostly boiled. One favorite meat is Cracow sausage, a special round, brown, very dry sausage, a delicacy with dark rye Polish bread and with beer. Other national dishes are *golabki*, cabbage leaves stuffed with minced meat and rice; *bigos*, sauerkraut with spicy meat and mushrooms; *flaki*, tripe served boiled or fried with carrots and onions; and *golonka*, pig's leg with horseradish and pease pudding.

Vegetables are usually potatoes, boiled or mashed, with french fries for foreign tourists, and cabbage, boiled or pickled as sauerkraut. Salads tend to be unimaginative: tomato sliced with onion, or plain lettuce, although better homes may produce cucumber in cream, grated beetroot, or wild forest mushrooms.

The foundation of Polish cuisine is old Slavic cooking. The Slavs used both sweet and sour cream to make their soups and gravies smooth and piquant as they do in Russian cooking. The widespread use of smoked bacon was typical of what was the East Prussian area of Poland. It was almost a sin if a housewife failed to brown her fried mashed-up potatoes in bacon fat, or to include it in a pot of dumplings. The flavor of smoked bacon and the tartness of sour cream are often blended together in festive roasts of veal or beef browned in bacon fat and sauced with cream.

Poles like pickled herring, with onions or in sour cream, particularly between glasses of vodka. In coastal and mountain homes, carp or trout may be on the menu as well, usually grilled whole to a crispy brown.

EATING OUT

Poles love sausages. Here a street vendor sells them grilled.

There is a wide selection of eating places. Quality used to vary from day to day as a result of varying food shortages, but today most foods are available—if one can afford them. Consistent high-quality dining is found only at the most expensive hotels and restaurants, which are open from late morning to mid-evening, and not usually later than about 9 p.m. Some don't open until 1 p.m. as alcohol may not be sold before that time. As in most of Europe, cafés are a way of life; in Poland these range from cheap soup kitchens where Poles munch grey bread sandwiches and drink bottles of very pungent beer, to hotdog stalls, Western-style fast food outlets, and milk bars often stocked with delicious pastries and ice creams. Warsaw has several Chinese restaurants and even a branch of McDonalds!

WARMING SOUPS

Soup is the start and glory of any good Polish meal. Polish soups range from a light and tasty transparent consommé to a rich creamy broth that almost forms a meal by itself. The most popular soup is *barszcz,* a clear beetroot soup often served

BIGOS

If there is a Polish national dish, it might well be *bigos*—a long-established favorite of cabbage, sauerkraut, onions, and a variety of meats—originally game but now mostly pork and sausage. It is eaten with mustard or very hot horseradish, and never chutney! This is a seasonal dish, as it relies on a supply of sauerkraut, the pickled cabbage made usually at summer's end to last through the winter. The following recipe for *bigos* is for six people, but if you can't get the sauerkraut and dried mushrooms it won't taste Polish at all!

    2 lb fresh sauerkraut
    9 oz cabbage, cut finely into strips
    5 oz chopped onions
    9 oz each of pork, beef, and sliced smoked sausage
    1.5 oz dried mushrooms
    1 teaspoon vegetable oil
    5 pimentos
    4 bay leaves
    1 clove of garlic
    salt, pepper, a little tomato paste

Boil the sauerkraut and fresh cabbage separately until tender. Cut the pork and beef into cubes; fry these in oil with the onions. Cook the mushrooms in boiling water once you have properly soaked them, then chop them finely. Now place everything into a large casserole dish with the seasonings; cover and cook over low heat for 90 minutes. *Note:* remove the bay leaves after 15 minutes, otherwise they will give too bitter a taste.

with such Polish favorites as sausage, cabbage, potatoes, sour cream, coarse rye bread, and beer. With the north coastline on the Baltic Sea and snow most winters, it is not surprising that Polish cuisine is geared to a cold, damp climate. There is a heavy emphasis on soups and meat, especially pork, as well as freshwater fish. Much use is made of cream, and pastries are often rich and delectable.

Poles enjoy *zurek*, a creamy white soup with sausage and potato, and *krupnik*, a thick soup made of barley and potato with pieces of bacon and carrots. Soups are often served with *pierogi*, small square pockets of dough filled with a cheesy potato mixture, or mushrooms or cabbage. *Pierogi* are filled with fruit or jam if they are served as dessert.

VODKA AND MORE

"The Poles are a moody people who take their fiery vodka in one violent gulp."

—*Godfrey Blunden in* Eastern Europe

For years Poles drank mostly at home, with hotel bars mainly for foreigners and for those addicted to alcohol. Today, bars are more popular as a cheerful part of city life.

Poland claims to have invented vodka, a claim hotly disputed by Russia. The drink probably originated in the 15th century when there was a decline in the supply of honey, the main ingredient of the traditional drink of mead. Somebody—either Polish or Russian—experimented by distilling alcohol from grain instead. In some such way, vodka was created. Poles drink it in small glasses, tossed straight back. There are many varieties such as those flavored with bison grass or juniper or wild cherry. The bottle is supposed to be empty before the guest leaves!

Beer is mostly bottled and there are several regional varieties. The two most popular brands are the strong tasting Tatra Pils and the lighter Piwo Zywiecki.

Many soft drinks are available too, with strawberry and apple being the most popular flavors. The better fruit juices are made from real fruit, though there are plenty of cheaper, more chemical concoctions available in cartons. Bottled Pepsi and Coke is available everywhere. Tap water is not always safe for drinking. Poles buy bottles of mineral water and there is usually one on the table at any meal.

Poland produces several varieties of vodka and beer. But there is no Polish wine.

Poles love tea. They drink tea (*herbata*) with everything, usually in glasses, without milk, and with lemon and heaps of sugar. Their coffee is a strong brew, reflecting the Turkish influence. It is made by pouring water over ground coffee in a glass or cup. Stirring is not advised, unless you want a mouthful of coffee grounds.

"A guest in the home, God in the home"

—famous old Polish proverb

Wild mushrooms are a delicacy, eaten fresh or dried. These mushrooms are found in the woods in the fall.

THE POLISH COOK

Through the centuries, the Polish housewife has learned to be frugal: she bottles fruit, pickles cabbage and onions, and dries the large, fragrant wild mushrooms. Not all homes, particularly in the country districts, have a refrigerator, so dried or preserved food is an important economy. Every village home has its own vegetable garden; town-dwellers often have an "allotment" of ground on the edge of town to grow food for the table. The woods are searched for blackberries or the blueberries that folk believe are a remedy for failing eyesight. Children gather them from the forests and sit beside the road, selling dark purple jars of berries.

The town housewife checks the prices in the supermarket, but prefers to buy from a local stall. In the Tatra foothills, the goat-milk cheese, brown-skinned and looking like a small loaf, is dry tasting and delicious.

In the old country homes, food is still cooked on a wood-burning stove topped with an iron plate. The fire below is arranged to provide different cooking temperatures on the top. The center is the hottest, for boiling water, and the edges cooler, for simmering soup. The oven section is above the cooking plate and is usually tiled round the sides. This will bake bread, roast meat, and heat the kitchen in winter.

Austria   A5

Baltic Sea   A1
Belarus   D2
Beskidy Range   C4
Bialystok   D2
Bielsko-Biala   B4
Bug   C2
Bydgoszcz   B2

Carpathian Mountains
   C4
Chelm   D3
Cracow   C4
Czech Republic   A4
Czestochowa   B3

Elblag   C1

Gdansk   B1
Gdansk   Bay B1
Gdynia   B1
Germany   A3
Gliwice   B4

Hungary   B5

Jelena Gora   A3

Katowice   B4
Kielce   C3

Lithuania   D1
Lodz   C3
Lublin   D3

Mazurian Lakes   C1

Neisse   A3

Oder   A2
Olsztyn   C2
Ostrowiec   C3

Plock   C2
Poznan   B2

Radom   C3
Russian Federation   C1

Rzeszow   C4

Silesia   B3
Slovakia   B5
Sopot   B1
Szczecin   A2

Torun   B2

Ukraine   D4

Vistula   B2

Walbrzych   B3
Warsaw   C2
Warta   A2
Wroclaw   B3

Zakopane   C4
Zielona Gora   A3

QUICK NOTES

CORRECT NAME
Rzeczpospolita Polska (Republic of Poland)

LAND AREA
120,728 square miles

POPULATION
38.3 million (1992)

CAPITAL
Warsaw

IMPORTANT CITIES
Cracow, Wroclaw, Katowice, Gdansk, Poznan

NATIONAL SYMBOL
White eagle

NATIONAL FLAG
White and red, halved horizontally

MAJOR RIVERS
Vistula, Oder (and Neisse)

MAJOR LAKES
Mazurian lakes

HIGHEST POINT
Rysy: 8,121 feet

NATIONAL/OFFICIAL LANGUAGE
Polish

MAJOR RELIGION
Roman Catholicism

CURRENCY
Zloty (U.S. $1 = 19,500 zloty)

MAIN EXPORTS
Coal, machinery, sulfur, chemicals, softwood timber, ships

IMPORTANT HOLIDAYS
May 3 (Constitution Day), November 11 (National Independence Day), and all major church festivals

IMPORTANT POLITICAL LEADERS
Josef Pilsudski (1867–1935)
Wladyslaw Sikorski (1881–1943)
Wladyslaw Gomulka (1905–1982)
Wojciech Jaruzelski (1923–)
Lech Walesa (1943–)

OTHER IMPORTANT FIGURES
Nicolaus Copernicus, astronomer (1473–1543)
Adam Mickiewicz, poet (1798–1855)
Frederic Chopin, composer (1810–1849)
Marie Curie, physicist (1867–1934)
Artur Rubinstein, pianist (1887–1982)
Stefan Wyszynski, cardinal (1901–1981)
Czeslaw Miloscz, writer (1911–)
Witold Lutoslawski, composer (1913–)

GLOSSARY

Arians   Believers of the doctrine of Arius, a 4th century Christian priest from Alexandria who preached that Christ was not of the same nature and essence as God.

cepelia   State-organized group of shops that buys traditionally-made goods from village workers and sells them.

collective farming   System where a number of farms are organized as a unit and worked by a community under the supervision of the state.

cooperative   Group or society owned and run jointly by its members with profits shared between them.

Gorale   Polish highlanders of the Tatra mountains.

icon   Holy picture or image that is venerated as sacred.

Iron Curtain   The barrier between the West and the former Soviet Union and its Communist allies.

Ł , ł   A special letter in the Polish alphabet pronounced like a "w." Words in this book that have this letter are: Wroclaw, Lodz, Wladyslaw, Jagiellonian, Pilsudski, Walesa, Wojtyla, Lowicz, Lutoslawski, Czeslaw Miloscz.

mass   Roman Catholic church service.

Politburo   Chief policy-making body of the Communist Party.

Resistance   An underground organization fighting for the liberty of their country, especially in World War II.

Sejm   Polish lower house of parliament.

Socialism   Belief that a country's wealth (for example, industry or land) should belong to the people as a whole and not to individuals.

BIBLIOGRAPHY

Bradley, John: *Eastern Europe*, Franklin Watts, New York, 1992.

Donica, Ewa and Sharman, Tim: *We Live in Poland*, Wayland, Hove, England, 1985.

Horn, Alfred and Pietras, Bozena (editors): *Insight Guides: Poland*, APA Publications, 1992.

Kaye, Tony: *Lech Walesa*, Chelsea House, New York, 1989.

INDEX

INDEX

INDEX